KINGDOM INVADERS

Postmodern Threats to
Biblical Christianity

God's blessings!
Randy Kennedy
Ecclesiastes 12:13

RANDY KENNEDY

xulon
PRESS

SOME KINGDOM COMMENTS...

"I found *Kingdom Invaders* to be thought provoking and passionate. Randy has been able to write about these 'thorny issues' in a conversational style which made for easy reading. Well done!"

Ric McClary, National Religious Broadcasters board member

"In his book, *Kingdom Invaders*, Randy Kennedy presents bold insight sorely lacking in our day. With uncompromising clarity, Randy chronicles, documents, and warns readers concerning crucial topics few dare to approach. May readers gain understanding and courage to resist the 'kingdom invaders' that face authentic Christians in these last days!"

Eric Barger, founder and director of Take a Stand! Ministries

"My friend Randy has poured his heart into this effort, and if you're seeking an honest and thought-provoking read, you will not be disappointed!"

Josh Heintzeman, state representative in the Minnesota House

TABLE OF CONTENTS

ACKNOWLEDGEMENTS

I first and foremost want to sincerely thank my Savior and Lord Jesus Christ for birthing in me the desire to write this book. Through the years of preparation and writing, and the times of excitement as well as discouragement, I continually felt His prompting to press on. He began this good work in me and was faithful in helping me complete it.

My wife Kristine was also a great encouragement when I experienced doubt. Many were the times that I questioned whether God was really in this project or not. She reminded me regularly of the distinct calling I had felt to write the book. And then I would continue on, once again assured that this was a task God had placed before me.

I thank my daughters, Stephanie and Valerie, for being precious gifts from God that softened my hard and selfish heart. Through them, I learned many of the spiritual lessons that I am now able to pass along in this book. They were also there to share treasured advice as I wrote.

Deep appreciation is reserved for my parents, Tom and Shirley, for the priceless blessing of being raised in a Christian home. They believed in me throughout the writing of this book and were there with the type of support that only loving parents can provide.

Finally, I offer my thanks to the staff at Xulon Press for their patient direction and encouragement. They educated this novice author in the difficult process of creating a book from start to finish. God used them as the conduit for bringing the important message He put on my heart to those who need to hear it.

INTRODUCTION

Tornadoes rarely strike urban centers. But in May 2012, densely-populated north Minneapolis was hit by a twister with winds of up to 135 mph. One person was killed, dozens were injured, and hundreds were left homeless. As you can imagine, the electrical infrastructure was hard hit and it literally took several days for all of the power to be restored.

The lack of electricity hindered the immediate recovery efforts and the power company came under criticism for the lengthy delay. A representative for the utility said that normally storm-related power outages affect a much smaller number of customers and repairs don't take very long. But in this case the damage was so significant they were having to restore power to one neighborhood at a time, focusing on areas with the most people first while the others would have to wait.

This story bears a striking similarity to what has been happening to Christianity in recent years. It used to be that the "storms" would come to the Church only occasionally, in manageable degrees of severity. False teachings and doctrine could be dealt with one issue at a time, either at a denominational level or throughout the universal Church, bringing a quick "repair" preventing their mainstream acceptance.

But today, we no longer have the convenience of repairing damage caused by one area of questionable doctrine at a time. The Kingdom of God is being pummeled by a great storm that has caused a "power outage" of historic proportions. The proper understanding of biblical truth is being severely damaged in so many areas that it seems virtually impossible to keep up with the necessary repairs. True Christians must now focus on the process of restoring foundational power to the Church as quickly as possible, with an emphasis on the false teachings that are affecting the most people, so the "recovery effort" can begin. That is the purpose of this book.

In October 2014, respected evangelical author Oz Guinness told an audience at a Family Research Council gathering in Washington D.C. that too many American Christians lack the "courage to be different and to clearly take a stand" in today's culture. Guinness in effect defined how postmodernism is threatening the Kingdom when he said believers have taken on the "comfortable relativism" of the society around them. He said this has done more to undermine Christianity "than all the persecutors in history put together." These are very strong words. And it makes it clear that I am not the only one who is deeply troubled by the worldliness that is invading the Kingdom today.

The thought of writing a book such as this was very intimidating to me. Although I did go to Bible college I'm far from a theologian or biblical scholar. (I have been an announcer in Christian radio for more than twenty years, so perhaps I've heard enough sermons that I deserve an honorary doctorate!) But because of many troubling conversations I've had recently with a variety of people who would call themselves Christians, I began to feel an overwhelming desire to address some of the most controversial questions in our American churches today — questions that at one time were not controversial at all.

Because of our Judeo-Christian culture, the answers found in the Bible were rarely questioned in previous generations. God's Word was understood, even by most who were not Christians, to be a credible guide to truth and wisdom. Even our founding fathers such as George Washington, Thomas Jefferson, and Ben Franklin spoke regularly of the importance of the Bible in guiding our steps — as individuals and as a fledgling nation. (Any doubt about this fact can be removed by checking out wallbuilders.com. Historian David Barton and his organization have done exhaustive research for several decades proving the biblical heritage of the United States.)

But in recent days, I have talked to more and more professed Christians who are expressing doubts about some of the very basics of the faith. It seems to be a symptom of a society that has grown increasingly skeptical of just about every statement of absolute fact. To today's "enlightened mind" it might sound naive, or even childlike, to look at the Bible the way our ancestors did — as unquestioned truth from God Himself.

I decided to title this book *Kingdom Invaders: Postmodern Threats to Biblical Christianity* because the Kingdom of God is under attack today as perhaps never before. God's Kingdom on earth is His Church, made up of His people. Many philosophies and theologies that at one time were understood to be dangerous and/or sinful were kept safely outside the walls of the Kingdom. But today, they are beginning to find breaches and are invading in increasing measure. As a result, many Christians are naively integrating these philosophies and theologies into their lives and churches, and the Kingdom is slowly being destroyed from within.

I realize this is not a new phenomenon. Most of the New Testament was written by Paul as he tried to defend the first century Church from the Kingdom invaders of that time. He wrote letter after letter, which we now call the Pauline epistles, to various churches he had founded on the truth of God but were later infiltrated by false teaching. His corrective letters have become a significant amount of the Scripture we look to for sound doctrine.

There was another time during the Middle Ages that a great deal of unbiblical teaching began to invade the Church. But God used a man named Martin Luther to point out the error and bring reformation.

So Kingdom invaders have always been around, but I believe today they are attacking with an end times fervor that is leading to greater and quicker destruction than ever before. I pray that one more time God will have mercy on His people and push back the invaders slipping through the breaches in the Kingdom walls.

x

Perhaps that is why I have felt led to write this book. It has been my experience that one of the toughest questions to answer is whether or not the promptings I feel in my heart are coming from my own desires and intellect, or from the direction and will of God. But if the idea for this book *is* from God, then perhaps it is because I share the innocent (and I would say wise) belief of previous generations that the Bible *can* be trusted, and its truths taken at face value.

Often when I have been asked the so-called controversial questions, whether with malice or sincerity, my first response has been, "What does the Bible say?" God's Word will be the source of the answers I share in these pages because, let's face it, without an absolute authority anything we believe about any of these issues would be merely opinion.

I realize that some Scripture is open for interpretation and I am of no illusion that everyone will completely agree with all of my conclusions. And please don't take offense at any given point and toss the book before you are finished reading it. I have spent countless hours praying, researching, and writing and I would hate for you to miss what God might want to say to you through these pages. I would only ask that you read with an open mind and then do what I have to do regularly — ask the Holy Spirit to give you wisdom and insight to know what God's truth really is, and then how He would want you to respond to that truth.

It was not my intention with this book to look at all of the invaders infiltrating the Church today, but rather, only those that have been the most insidious. Like spies passing through a breach in the middle of the night, these invaders have been able to bring their influence into the Kingdom almost unnoticed until the damage has quietly been done.

My goal is to live a life consecrated to the Lord, and perhaps the fact that you are reading this book means that you share that goal. Whatever the reason, I'm thankful that you are coming alongside me in this journey to find out what the Bible has to say about some of the most important issues facing Christianity today.

My prayer is that you will choose to join me in the battle against the invaders attempting to bring corruption and destruction into the Kingdom of God.

1–THE BIBLE:
CREDIBLE OR CORRUPTED?

There have been many people throughout history who have tried to prove the Word of God to be fraudulent, but none have been successful. And they never will, because absolute truth can't be proven to be a lie.

T hrough my many years of studying the Bible — as well as its related history, archeology, and other sciences — I have come to a point where I can confidently say, "It's true that you can't prove the Bible to be absolute truth, but you can get oh-so-close!" Much of the postmodern threat to Christianity today starts with a lack of belief in the Bible as the inerrant Word of God, His heart and mind revealed to us. So before anything else, I want to share solid proofs that the Bible can be trusted as a credible source of absolute truth and guidance; a book that is more than mere suggestion for how we should live our lives.

In 2 Timothy 3:16-17 it says:

All Scripture is God-breathed and is useful for teaching, rebuking, correcting and training in righteousness, so that the man of God may be thoroughly equipped for every good work.

When the remarkable evidence supporting the infallibility of the Bible is presented it is clear that this is more than just a hollow claim.

PROVEN CREDIBILITY

There have been many people throughout history who have tried to prove the Word of God to be fraudulent, but none have been successful. And they never will, because absolute truth can't be proven to be a lie. Among the most well-known cases are two men who in recent years gathered evidence in their separate attempts to bring into question the credibility of the Bible, and Christianity as a whole.

Josh McDowell was a self-proclaimed agnostic who had a tragic childhood which included an abusive, alcoholic father and years of sexual abuse by a man who worked for his family. Because of his resulting bitterness, McDowell gladly took on an assignment as a college student to disprove the claims of Christianity.

Lee Strobel was an atheist who was working as a journalist at the Chicago Tribune. After his wife accepted Jesus as her Savior, Strobel set out to systematically prove Christianity to be a fraud using the skills he learned in law school and as an investigative reporter.

Rather than exposing the claims found in God's Word to be a lie, both men actually became Christians because of the indisputable truth they uncovered. McDowell wrote about his experiences in a book called *Evidence that Demands A Verdict*,[1] and a follow-up, *More Evidence that Demands a Verdict*.[2] Strobel has written several books detailing his findings, including *The Case for Christ*[3] and *The Case for Faith*.[4]

What are some of the ways we can know the Bible to be actual truth from God Himself? Amazingly, it was written over the course of sixteen hundred years by more than forty different authors from all walks of life — and yet a common thread is woven throughout. This could not have been the work of men alone. To be included in the Holy Bible, the various books had to be recognized as inspired by a council of rabbis and councils of church leaders after passing a test of careful guidelines.

As the Scriptures were written, the original manuscripts were meticulously copied by Jewish scribes. If they made even one error, the manuscript was buried and they had to start over. Can you imagine such a process today? As I'm typing these words into my computer, I can't fathom even at this early point in the book having to stop, bury what I've already done, and start over all because I made a single mistake. But that is what the scribes faced because of the importance they placed on preserving the Scriptures in their exact form. They understood them to be truth from God and treated them as such.

There is remarkable evidence that the Bible we have today is true to the original writings. More than fifty-three hundred ancient hand-made manuscripts still exist. In fact, during the 1900's alone, more than one hundred Bible manuscripts were found in Egypt. Among the most amazing discoveries occurred in 1947. The Dead Sea Scrolls were located in some caves in what is now called the West Bank of Israel.

Many of the hundreds of scrolls were found as small scraps that had to be meticulously and painstakingly reassembled over several years. They contained some of the earliest Old Testament manuscripts ever found, over one thousand years older than most of those previously used for Bible translation. With the exception of very minor differences such as the spellings of some words, the scrolls were virtually identical to the later hand-written Old Testament copies — proof that the Bible we use today has been preserved without corruption!

DIGGING A LITTLE DEEPER

The discovery of the Dead Sea Scrolls hints at another convincing evidence that the Bible is really truth from God — archeological proofs. Not one discovery has been unearthed that has ever disproved any aspect of the Bible. On the contrary, Christians have been able to wait with anticipation every time a dig is planned in the land where biblical history was written. As I once heard an evangelist put it: "You can't turn over a spate of dirt in Israel without proving the accuracy of the Bible." The same can be said for the entire region highlighted in God's Word.

The Rose Publishing book *Why Trust the Bible?* documents fifty Old Testament and fifty New Testament archeological discoveries that should be impossible for skeptics to ignore.[5] For example, "horned altars" made of stone have been uncovered in the area of the biblical cities of Dan and Beersheba. These altars, which date to about the tenth century BC, were referred to in the Old Testament at least twenty times.

In another remarkable example, an inscription was found on stone at the city of Dan by archeologists in the early 1990's containing the Aramaic expression "the house of David" and references to King David's descendants. This was a very significant discovery, because up to that point no non-biblical reference to one of Israel's most important historical leaders had ever been found. This silenced many critics who for a long time had said the biblical account of a King David had to be mere fiction.

Many have argued that the account of Noah and the ark is just a fable and could never really have happened. But archeologists have uncovered significant non-biblical evidence for a worldwide flood. *The Gilgamesh Epic*, which dated to the seventh century BC, was found in Ninevah on a series of baked clay tablets. It includes a flood story remarkably similar to the account of Noah and his family found in Genesis 6-9. Similar archeological discoveries throughout the region make a strong argument for the accuracy of this historic event as recorded in the Bible.

More recent evidence testifies to the fact of a worldwide flood as well. Fossils of sea creatures have been found in the Grand Canyon, hundreds of miles inland and more than a mile above sea level. Across the world in Asia fossilized shellfish have been located in the Himalayas, the highest mountain region in the world. Did you catch that? Fossilized sea creatures in the highest mountain region in the world! I think you would have to agree, this is something that could only have happened if the entire world was at one time covered with water.

There is one more thing I'd like you to think about in relation to fossils. I have lived in a rural area for many years and have seen lots of road kill. In all the years I've been here, I have never seen a dead animal ever come close to becoming a fossil. The carcass is usually gone, bones and all, within a couple of weeks. Every available scavenger takes advantage of the opportunity, and that poor dead creature becomes a wilderness buffet until it is completely gone.

So how do dead animals become fossils? They would have to be buried quickly before they could succumb to scavengers or natural decay. There are very few things that could cause the soil to so rapidly cover these animals. But among them — you may have already guessed it — would be a catastrophic flood such as the one in Noah's day.

One other foundational Bible story has come into question over the last several decades. There have been many noted archaeologists who have said there is no evidence of a huge exodus of Hebrew slaves from Egypt as described in the Old Testament book of Exodus. But in recent days, researchers have found that there is in fact much archaeological evidence to support the Bible's historical account of the enslavement of the Jewish people in Egypt — as well as their subsequent release.

This research has been documented in the Tim Mahoney book and film, *Patterns of Evidence: The Exodus*.[6] According to Mahoney, the confusion has come from the fact that the evidence has been discovered in a subterranean period a couple of hundred years prior to what has been traditionally believed to be the time of the Exodus. The question then has to be asked: if the biblical account of this historic event is supported by archeology, shouldn't the traditional time line be brought into question rather than the accuracy of the Bible?

The credibility of New Testament history has also been well proven through archeology. One of the most eye-popping discoveries occurred in 1961 when a stone unearthed by archeologists at the ruins of Caesarea Maratima in Israel was inscribed with the name of Pontius Pilate, one of the Roman officials involved in the crucifixion of Jesus. As one would expect, the inscription dates to the time of Christ.

Another inscription found at a dig in 1929 is about as close to smoking-gun evidence as one can get to proving the historical accuracy of the Bible. Archeologists uncovered a stone near Corinth in Greece that contained the name of Erastus, and noted that he was a Roman public official. In Romans 16:23, while writing from Corinth almost nineteen centuries earlier, Paul refers to an Erastus by name and notes his position as — guess what — a public official! Please don't miss the significance of this. I'm not referring to a made-for-TV movie plot line here. This stone was found in real life by real people and actually drew a modern day connection to a real person from New Testament history. Amazing!

One prominent archeologist noted that the book of Luke references thirty-two countries, fifty-four cities, and nine islands without making a single geographic mistake — not one. If Luke's first century GPS was that precise, is there any reason to doubt the accuracy of his biographical and historical accounts?

Luke gives the most detailed description of the circumstances surrounding the birth of Jesus, which includes an account of a census in Luke 2:1-7. To complete the census the Romans required citizens under their rule, including the Jews, to return to the place of their birth to be counted. Remarkably, archeologists have uncovered ancient census forms showing that those who had moved out of their province of birth were required by the Romans to return to their homelands to be counted — just as Luke described some two thousand years ago.

Do you see a pattern developing here? These are not vague discoveries that could be interpreted in a variety of ways. These are documented archaeological finds that point very specifically and accurately to people and events recorded in the Bible.

ANCIENT PROPHETIC PROOF

This moves us to what I believe to be the most compelling proof that the Bible is truly the Word of God — the literally hundreds of prophecies that have been fulfilled. Most of the Old Testament prophecies referred to the coming Messiah — the anticipated deliverer of a Jewish people that had been repeatedly oppressed by foreign powers. No less than 109 prophecies about the Messiah were fulfilled by Jesus. Among the most well-known related to His birth:

Prophecy	O.T. Reference	N.T. Fulfillment
A Child will be born	Isaiah 9:6	Luke 2:11
He will be born of a virgin	Isaiah 7:13,14	Luke 1:26-35
He will be from the bloodline of David	Isaiah 9:7	Matthew 1:1
He will be from the tribe of Judah	Genesis 49:8-10	Matthew 1:1-3
He will be of the seed of Abraham	Genesis 17:7,8	Matthew 1:1,17
He will be born in Bethlehem	Micah 5:2-5	Matthew 2:1-6
Kings will bring gifts and bow down to Him	Psalm 72:10,11	Matthew 2:1-11
There will be a massacre of children	Jeremiah 31:15	Matthew 2:16-18

Considering how long it took for these prophecies to be fulfilled reinforces how remarkable they really are. The prophecies in Genesis were written more than twelve hundred years before the birth of Jesus, the prophecy from the Psalms more than eight hundred years prior to His birth, and the remaining listed prophecies were each penned more than five hundred years before Jesus was born.

I'm no math genius, but those who *are* say the probability of these eight prophecies being accidentally fulfilled by one man would be one chance in one-hundred-million-billion. That's a one followed by seventeen zeros! Add in the rest of the messianic prophecies and the mathematical probability that Jesus could have accidentally fulfilled them all would probably fill up this page with zeros.

In the natural, such fulfilled prophecies are obviously hard for the mind to accept. They are so accurate that some skeptics have reasoned the Old Testament accounts had to have been written after the fact, so as to fit the events they supposedly were predicting. But this belief is made irrelevant when one considers the Septuagint. This was a translation of the Old Testament from the original Hebrew and Aramaic languages into Greek. It was translated by Jewish scholars between 250 BC and 100 BC into the language of the dominant world power at that time, Greece. The abbreviation BC stands for "Before Christ," so thanks to the Septuagint we can know without a doubt that the Old Testament prophecies concerning Jesus *were* written well before His birth.

Just as an aside, I've always thought the fact that our calendar years are based on the time of Christ's birth was proof enough that He was the most important person to ever walk the face of the earth. But there has been a concerted effort in recent years to replace BC and AD (an abbreviation of the Greek words "anno Domini" which in English is "in the year of our Lord") with BCE and CE. This stands for "Before the Common Era" and "the Common Era." As senseless as this sounds, the move has gained steam and could soon be the norm on the calendars in our increasingly postmodern society.

Another way skeptics have attempted to explain away the dramatic accuracy of the Old Testament messianic prophecies is to say that Jesus lived His life in such a way as to "fit into" the prophecies. This could have been the case in some instances, such as when he rode into Jerusalem on a donkey as recorded in three of the Gospels and prophesied in Zechariah 9:9. But this argument is easily defeated when you consider that Jesus could have done nothing to fulfill the previously mentioned prophecies relating to his birth, or for that matter, the prophecies relating to His death. Among them:

Prophecy	O.T. Reference	N.T. Fulfillment
He will be despised and rejected	Isaiah 53:2-3	Luke 23:18
He will be hung on a "tree" as a curse	Deuteronomy 21:23	Galatians 3:13
His hands and feet will be pierced	Psalm 22:16	John 20:25-29
Not one of His bones will be broken	Psalm 34:20	John 19:31-36
His body will be pierced	Zechariah 12:10	John 19:34-37
Soldiers will cast lots for His clothing	Psalm 22:18	John 19:23-24
He will be buried with the rich	Isaiah 53:9	Matthew 27:57-60
He will be raised from the dead	Psalm 16:8-11	John 2

For those who doubt the biblical account of the crucifixion, death, and resurrection of Jesus, one need not look further than the lives of the twelve apostles after Jesus ascended into heaven (Acts 1:9-11). Each of these men, with the exception of John, died a violent death defending the truth that Jesus sacrificed His life on a cross for our sins. These were the same men who prior to His death scattered in fear when Jesus was arrested at Gethsemane. Later that same night, Peter famously denied knowing Jesus three times because he feared for his life.

What changed these men from timid believers to courageous martyrs? It would be ridiculous to think they would give their lives knowing full well that Jesus' resurrection was a lie. On the contrary, when He died and rose to life again, the apostles had numerous personal encounters with the risen Christ. They were left with no doubt that Jesus was who He said He was — the Son of God. And they lived the rest of their days to spread His message, regardless of the persecution that faced them, knowing their eternal reward would be worth it all.

MODERN PROPHETIC PROOF

Probably the most amazing fulfillment of biblical prophecy relates to the nation of Israel. The Jewish people were dispersed from their homeland and scattered across the earth some two thousand years ago. And over these many centuries, they have been a persecuted group of people. This fulfills a prophecy found in Deuteronomy 28:64-67:

Then the Lord will scatter you among all nations, from one end of the earth to the other...Among those nations you will find no repose, no resting place for the sole of your foot. There the Lord will give you an anxious mind, eyes weary with longing, and a despairing heart. You will live in constant suspense, filled with dread both day and night, never sure of your life. In the morning you will say, "If only it were evening!" and in the evening, "If only it were morning!" – because of the terror that will fill your hearts and the sights that your eyes will see.

This horror for the Jewish people hit its peak during the World War II holocaust when about six million of them were exterminated. Out of this devastation however came the most remarkable fulfilled prophecy of them all, from Ezekiel 37, culminating in verses 12 and 14:

Therefore prophesy and say to them: 'This is what the Sovereign Lord says: O my people, I am going to open your graves and bring you up from them; I will bring you back to the land of Israel. I will put my Spirit in you and you will live, and I will settle you in your own land'...

Incredibly, in 1948 Israel became a nation once again, just as prophesied by Ezekiel around 580 BC. Perhaps the most amazing thing about this is the fact that no people group in history has ever come together again after being scattered for two thousand years. And through all those centuries, the Jewish people actually kept their distinct identity as prophesied in Jeremiah 31:35-36:

This is what the Lord says, he who appoints the sun to shine by day, who decrees the moon and stars to shine by night, who stirs up the sea so that its waves roar–the Lord Almighty is his name: "Only if these decrees vanish from my sight," declares the Lord, "will the descendants of Israel ever cease to be a nation before me."

In other words, as long as the sun, moon, and stars remain in the sky, and the waves of the seas continue to roar with their powerful beauty, the Jews will remain a distinct people — a nation before the Lord. Clearly, their preservation as a race can only realistically be explained supernaturally.

Why would I say that? The great melting pot of the United States provides a terrific example. Residents of the U.S. have ancestors that have come from all over the world. I am of mostly Irish descent, yet like most people in our country I would identify myself as American through and through. My wife is of largely German ancestry, so together we typify the average American family — mixed blood, mixed heritage. Of course, our two daughters have more mixed blood than we do, and their children will likely have an ancestry that varies even greater still. We have assimilated into the culture of our nation and have no compelling desire to return and live in our "homelands" of Ireland and Germany, because we consider our homeland to be the United States.

But the Jewish people have managed to maintain their heritage and, in large part, their distinct bloodline for twenty centuries. This is despite the fact that they had been scattered across the world in various countries with many diverse cultures. Today, Jews continue to move to Israel by the thousands every year drawn by an overwhelming supernatural desire to be in their homeland with their own people — all conforming to biblical prophecy.

One final thought considering the modern nation of Israel. Isn't it interesting that year in and year out this tiny little nation is in the news? Its population is similar to Tajikistan, Switzerland, Austria, and Honduras, and yet you rarely hear anything newsworthy coming out of these nations. When you stop and think about it, it makes absolutely no sense in the natural that the world is fixated on Israel, a nation about the size of Virginia with a population at the time of this writing that is slightly less than that of New York City.

It's almost comical to hear reports about the next "peace talks" scheduled between Israel and...you name the Arab nation or people group (most often the Palestinians). This has literally been going on as long as I can remember. The headlines relating to Israel today sound like the headlines from last year, and from the last decade, and from twenty years ago, etc. It's almost as if Israel and the Jewish people are somehow special. Of course, through the Scriptures we know they *are* special — God's chosen people, the apple of His eye. (We'll explore this more in chapter four.)

QUESTIONS ABOUT CONTRADICTIONS

There are some who have come to question the credibility of the Bible based on its perceived contradictions. But in context with the rest of Scripture, they aren't contradictions at all. For an example, let's take a look at several passages relating to prayer that will give us an apparent contradiction followed by the clarification.

In Matthew 21:22 Jesus says: "If you believe, you will receive whatever you ask for in prayer." And again in Matthew 7:7-8: "Ask and it will be given to you; seek and you will find; knock and the door will be opened to you. For everyone who asks receives; he who seeks finds; and to him who knocks, the door will be opened."

Have you received everything you have asked for in prayer? Neither have I. But the person who would say these verses bring into question the credibility of the Bible serves to highlight the danger that comes from taking Scripture out of context. A skeptical person could say, "God doesn't answer all of my prayers so this Christianity thing must be bogus." But in context with the rest of the Bible we know there are certain prerequisites that must be met in order to have an effective prayer life. Among them: there must be true belief in God and His ability to answer prayers.

In James 1:6-7 it says: "But when he asks, he must believe and not doubt, because he who doubts is like a wave of the sea, blown and tossed by the wind. That man should not think he will receive anything from the Lord..." While this verse is specifically talking about those who ask God for wisdom, it is a principle that applies universally — that a lack of faith in God hinders our prayers.

God also requires the person who is praying to have a heart of sincerity, desiring to please Him. Psalm 37:4 says: "Delight yourself in the Lord and he will give you the desires of your heart." And again in Matthew 7:33: "But seek first his kingdom and his righteousness, and all these things will be given to you as well." A person who desires to please God in all he does will have properly focused prayers with selfless motives.

Conversely, it says in James 4:3: "When you ask, you do not receive, because you ask with wrong motives, that you may spend what you get on your pleasures." We also see in Proverbs 15:29: "The Lord is far from the wicked but he hears the prayer of the righteous."

This verse transitions us to another prerequisite — a personal effort to live in obedience to God. In 1 John 3:21-22 we read: "Dear friends, if our hearts do not condemn us, we have confidence before God and receive from him anything we ask, because we obey his commands and do what pleases him."

So we can see that an effective prayer life depends greatly on having a heart devoted to God and then doing our best to live in right relationship with Him. These things are our responsibility.

But there is one prerequisite that trumps everything else — our prayers have to be in keeping with the will of God. We cannot expect any request we bring that is outside of His will to be answered affirmatively. As it says in 1 John 5:14: "This is the confidence we have in approaching God: that if we ask anything according to his will, he hears us."

Jesus Himself gave a perfect example of this at Gethsemane prior to His crucifixion in Matthew 26:39: "Going a little farther, he fell with his face to the ground and prayed, 'My Father, if it is possible, may this cup be taken from me. Yet not as I will, but as you will.'" We all know the outcome of this petition. God answered "no" to the prayer of His only Son because the result was crucial to His plan of salvation for the world.

So the seeming contradictions in the Bible, when taken in context, are really not contradictions at all. On the contrary, as with our example on prayer, when examining the full counsel of God they actually provide a broader understanding of His heart and mind.

NEW VERSIONS OF THE OLD TRUTH

There are some people who are troubled by the fact that there are now many different versions of the Bible. They are of the faulty assumption that these are various reinterpretations of the original Bible and therefore must be corrupted. This belief has become more of an issue in recent decades. Until the early twentieth century, the King James Version of the Bible had been the prominent translation that virtually every Christian grew up with for more than three hundred years. (Even this version went through occasional updates to reflect the changes in language over time.)

But the knowledge gained from the many newly discovered manuscripts early in the 1900's led to numerous modern versions, each trying to more closely reflect the true meaning of the original texts while being as readable as possible. Keep in mind that although there are many different versions of the Bible today, they are translations — not reinterpretations — and they all attempt to remain true to the language contained in the original Hebrew, Aramaic, and Greek Scriptures.

There are exceptions to be aware of. The Joseph Smith Translation is among reinterpretations to be avoided. Named after the founder of the Mormon religion and the one who made the revisions, Smith said his "inspired version" corrected the corruption found in every other translation. Even though he never learned the original languages of the Bible, Smith made thousands of changes to the King James Version. Another false religion, the Jehovah's Witnesses, use a reinterpreted "Bible" as well called the New World Translation which meshes with their unique doctrines. (We will learn more about the beliefs of the Mormons and Jehovah's Witnesses in chapter ten.)

Some of the more common versions available today that are safe and can be trusted include the Revised Standard, American Standard, New American Standard, Today's English, the original New International, New King James, and New Living just to name a few.

CONCLUDING THOUGHT

There are simply no other "holy books" used by any other religion that have provable authenticity like the Bible. On the contrary, archeology and other sciences have actually proven these other books to be contradictory and inaccurate at best, complete frauds at worst. And none of these other books can claim fulfillment of even a single specific prophecy, whereas literally hundreds of Bible prophecies have been, and continue to be, fulfilled.

What I have written in this chapter is really just the tip of the iceberg in terms of showing the Bible to be credible as the Word of God, worthy of our belief in its accuracy and infallibility. With this understanding, we can move forward knowing that the Scriptures can be trusted to help us in discerning whether the philosophies and theologies being advanced today are based on sound doctrine, or are actually invaders of the Kingdom.

2–THE BIBLE:
LITERAL OR LITERARY?

As I read the creation account, it dawned on me that all God had to do was speak the words and this massive, complex universe was formed. An incredible reality then hit me like a lightning bolt — absolutely nothing is impossible with God! That's the understanding you develop when you believe in a literal interpretation of the Scriptures.

The passage of Scripture mentioned at the beginning of the last chapter from 2 Timothy 3:16-17 appears to make it quite clear that the Bible is to be considered more than just a good book containing literary classics. Unfortunately, many who would call themselves Christians today think of the Bible in just that way — a piece of intriguing literature worthy of being known intellectually but hardly absolute truth.

This way of thinking is not new. It actually started right at the beginning of human history. In Genesis 3:1 the serpent, who was indwelt by Satan, asked Eve the question, "Did God really say...?" This was his way of getting Eve to doubt whether God meant what He said when He gave a commandment. Both Eve and Adam believed Satan's lie and disobeyed God.

The tactic Satan used in the Garden of Eden was effective then, and has been effective to this day when those who call themselves Christians ignore what God's Word has to say on certain issues. People will read clear biblical teaching and then Satan plants a thought in their minds, "Did God really say...?" The next thing you know they become accepting of, or even participate in, disobedience to God's Word. (By the way, if you question whether Satan really exists, that topic is covered in chapter four.)

THE ORIGINS OF DOUBT, THE DOUBT OF ORIGINS

The question of whether or not to take the Bible literally took on new life in the 1800's when Charles Darwin and the theory of evolution began to gain credibility in the scientific community of the day. Because his theories appeared to be based on science, many Christians started to feel that their Bible-based creation theology must either be flawed, or the result of misinterpretation. So it was thought that in order for belief in Christianity to remain viable, evolutionary ideology had to be somehow integrated into the Bible's account of creation.

The first time I did a serious creation study it was a real eye opener for me. Prior to that, my finite mind had always put limits on God. Without wanting to admit it, I wondered if He could really know my thoughts and hear my prayers among the seven billion or so people on earth. Could He really be directly involved in the lives of all people? And could He really know the end from the beginning as it says in Isaiah 46:10?

But as I read the creation account, it dawned on me that all God had to do was speak the words and this massive, complex universe was formed. An incredible reality then hit me like a lightning bolt — absolutely *nothing* is impossible with God! All those stories in the Bible that seemed so outrageous before — Noah and the flood, the parting of the Red Sea, Jonah and the whale, the many healings, and people being raised from the dead — all of a sudden seemed very plausible. There is nothing too hard for the God who created all we see by merely speaking a few words. That's the understanding you develop when you believe in a literal interpretation of the Scriptures.

29

What happens when you doubt that? In a best case scenario, God's power is diminished in your mind and the Bible becomes less authoritative from Genesis to Revelation. In a worst case scenario, you start believing God doesn't really exist and the Bible becomes meaningless.

God's Word gives a clear account of how the earth and universe were created. So why do so many scientists and Christians accept evolution as fact? If you grew up attending public schools like me, I would imagine you experienced the same thing I did in science class. Evolution was taught without any question as to its credibility, and we saw all the drawings and read the books that told us we evolved from apes. With such intelligent and respected people as teachers and textbook writers telling us these things, it was easy to question what we were being taught by the volunteers who led our Sunday school classes.

As a result, the theory of evolution is almost never presented as anything but fact today. Wherever information is disseminated or traded — be it the classroom, workplace, or in the media (including taxpayer-supported public broadcasting) — any scientific discussion is interpreted through an evolutionary lens. Even the interpretive centers and tour guides at our state and national parks explain everything using an evolutionary model. So this belief ends up becoming self-perpetuating. We learned it as kids, so it becomes integrated into our thinking and then is naturally woven into our lives. Eventually it becomes fact in our minds without any thought of questioning its validity, and the mere theory is perceived as reality throughout an entire culture.

So virtually everyone who lives in our country today has been influenced by a lifetime of indoctrination telling us there has to be something to evolutionary concepts. Some less than reputable politicians are fond of saying that if you tell a lie often enough, with enough conviction, it becomes truth in people's minds. That is exactly what has happened with the theory of evolution. But if you begin to read the Bible from the very first verse putting aside all preconceived ideas, then incorporating evolutionary thought into the creation account just doesn't work.

THE EARTH: JUST A KID?

I am what would be considered a young-earth creationist. I believe that when you accept the Genesis account of creation and take it at face value, and then throw in the Old and New Testament genealogies for good measure, you will come to the conclusion that the earth (and universe for that matter) is only about six thousand years old.

Although the biblical genealogies may seem boring and unimportant when you read them, they actually establish a very important time line that supports the view of a relatively young universe. And even though scientific methods such as carbon dating would occasionally indicate that certain matter is much older than that, it's important to note that this method has been found to be notoriously flawed at times. I won't go into detail, but suffice it to say it relies heavily on certain presumptions that can seriously skew its outcomes.

I am only bringing up this age issue because there are many Christians who believe in the evolutionary idea that the universe is billions of years old. When I talk with these people, they say it really doesn't matter one way or another what you believe on the subject; it is not necessary to believe in a young earth in order to be saved. This is true. But I often find that these are some of the same people who say other scriptural truths aren't all that important, like whether or not the virgin birth of Jesus actually happened, or if He truly died on a cross and rose again. These things *are* absolutely crucial to the Gospel and necessary beliefs for salvation.

ORIGIN THEORIES

Most people today have at least heard of the Gap Theory of creation. In order to make Genesis 1 fit into evolutionary theory, some well-meaning Christians developed a belief that there was likely a gap of billions of years between verses 2 and 3:

> Now the earth was formless and empty, darkness was over the surface of the deep, and the Spirit of God was hovering over the waters. And God said, "Let there be light," and there was light.

But when you read these verses without any preconceived ideas, it is very clear this is simply one continuous commentary. It's a real stretch to believe anything else. Without the verse numbers included in the text, it is even hard to distinguish where verse 2 ends and verse 3 begins. Besides, when you think of God's reason for birthing a physical creation — to have fellowship with His people — what would be His purpose for putting a formless, void, dark planet such as earth in the universe and then just leaving it that way for billions of years? It makes absolutely no sense.

If these verses are read as one continuous thought, God immediately began the process of bringing order to the earth during that first glorious day of creation. Since the sun was not created until the fourth day, God's light filled the earth until then. The same will happen again at the end of time when the New Heaven and the New Earth will be illuminated only by the glory of God (Revelation 21:23).

Another origin belief, the Day-Age Theory, says that the six days of creation in the Bible are not actually literal days, but rather, periods of time. The Hebrew word translated as "day" in the Old Testament can be used to represent a period of time as well as a twenty-four hour day, so this provided another opportunity to incorporate evolution into the creation account. But again, if you take the Scriptures at face value as written, it becomes clear that the days of creation are literal twenty-four hour periods. In context with the rest of the Bible nothing else makes sense.

In Genesis 1:3-5, God himself established the concept of the twenty-four hour day when he separated light from darkness and called them "day" and "night." And it's apparent the Holy Spirit knew the matter would eventually come into question, because He inspired the author of Genesis — Moses — to write the words, "there was evening, and there was morning – the first day." These words are used to complete the description of all six days of creation making it quite unreasonable to believe these were anything but literal twenty-four hour periods.

The Sabbath day that we are instructed to honor puts an exclamation point on the belief in twenty-four hour creation days. The fourth of the Ten Commandments found in Exodus 20:9-11 and Deuteronomy 5:12-15 says that "in six days the Lord made the heavens and the earth, the sea and all that is in them, and rested on the seventh day; therefore the Lord blessed the Sabbath day and made it holy." Is there any doubt that this is referring to literal, twenty-four hour days? Unless you're trying to put a square peg into a round whole, the answer is an emphatic, "No!" The Sabbath, which was established by God at the time of creation, has been understood throughout all of human history to mean a twenty-four hour day of rest at the end of a seven-day week.

DECEPTIVELY YOUNG

One reason some people give for believing the earth is billions of years old has to do with how old things look when they are in their natural state, such as rocks. And what about creatures such as certain reptiles that look so prehistoric. In my opinion, these questions are easily answered.

First of all, it is only an assumption that rocks appear to be old. For example, certain formations and erosional features in the Grand Canyon that were thought to be millions of years old, are already being observed in the area of Mount St. Helens, Washington following its cataclysmic earthquake and volcanic eruption in 1980. In fact, a formation at the base of the mountain is so similar to the Grand Canyon that it has been referred to as the "Little Grand Canyon." This was created quickly after a small catastrophic event. Generally, creation scientists believe the big

Grand Canyon was formed about four thousand years ago as the result of a major catastrophic event — the flood of Noah's day.

In another example, it's been said by some evolutionary scientists that stalagmites and stalactites, which are mineral formations found in underground caverns, take millions of years to develop. But underneath the marble floor of the Lincoln Memorial, which was built in 1922, stalactites up to five feet in length were found in the 1960's. By commonly-used calculations, these should have taken about sixty thousand years to form, instead of just forty. So as you can see, preconceived assumptions and reality are not always the same thing.

Whenever you hear people refer to animals such as reptiles as prehistoric creatures because of their appearance, take pause for a moment and think about that. Just because they have perceived similarities to dinosaurs, doesn't mean their ancestors are millions or billions of years old. Their skin may look old, but really that's just a perception. Our skin is probably older than what is on most of the reptiles we see on TV or at the zoo. Don't let evolutionary indoctrination keep you from recognizing the truth. Based on Scripture, all fish, birds, and land animals were created during days five and six of the creation week along with Adam.

I know some people are tripped up by the fact that dinosaurs don't appear to be mentioned in the Bible. But this is not a problem. The term "dinosaur" wasn't used to describe this particular genus of creatures until the 1840's. It was invented by English scientist Sir Richard Owen using two Greek words which together mean "fearfully great lizard." Prior to that, dinosaurs were described regularly in the ancient writings of many cultures as "dragons." This includes accounts of men seeing and killing them. In other words, dinosaurs and humans did coexist for a time on earth.

Interestingly, two creatures mentioned in the Old Testament book of Job — the behemoth in chapter 40 and the leviathan in chapter 41 — were massive according to their description. It is not a stretch to believe that these were among the supposedly prehistoric dinosaurs which were alive during Job's lifetime, roughly 2,000 BC.

Most of the creatures in the dinosaur genus became extinct a few thousand years ago, just as to this day, certain animal species become extinct for various reasons every year. Those ancient-looking reptiles you might see on TV or in a zoo are no more prehistoric than any other animals alive today. They just happen to bear similarities to what we believe the dinosaurs looked like.

One final thought has to be addressed concerning the evolutionary belief about dinosaurs. If they existed millions of years before man populated the earth, then how could they have become extinct? After all, the Bible tells us that death did not enter the world until it was introduced through the sin of Adam and Eve (Romans 5:12). This is an inescapable question that has no answer when trying to reconcile evolutionary belief with the truth found in the Bible.

THE CASE FOR QUILLS AND CLAWS

There are some who have difficulty accepting the biblical account of creation because of the fact that animals are regularly equipped with "defense and attack structures." Examples of defense structures include the quills on a porcupine or the smell of a skunk that keep predators at bay. Attack structures include the claws used by a cat to catch and hold its prey, or the unbelievable speed of one of those cats, the cheetah, for chasing down a delicious meal. (The muscular structure and aerodynamic design of a cheetah would rival any Indy series car!)

Design and attack structures would seem to contradict the biblical account that these animals were created before the world became corrupted by sin. After all, there would be no death — including animals attacking other animals — before the fall of man. So why were animals designed this way?

I believe there is really a very simple explanation. As with so many other things, Jesus is where we can find the answer. God knows the end from the beginning (Isaiah 46:10) so He knew Adam and Eve would succumb to temptation. Therefore, even before the creation of the world, God had already prepared a Savior — His son Jesus — to redeem mankind from the curse of sin. Just as He knew people would need a Savior, God was acutely aware that animals would need preparation to live in a sin-sick world. So at the time of creation He gave them the defense and attack structures they would eventually need for survival.

TRUE BEGINNINGS

Evolutionists of course have a very different take on all of this, including how the universe began. Their most common explanation is the well-known "Big Bang Theory." Without going too deeply into it, this theory says everything that we see got its start with a "primordial soup" that began expanding through some source of energy. Then all it took for everything to take on the complexity and order that we see today was time — several billion years to be exact. Now time does have some positive attributes, such as healing wounds and broken hearts, but magical it is not. It doesn't matter how much time is allotted — whether one day or a billion years — nothing ever becomes more complex and ordered by itself without a creator or designer.

Metals, for example, are mined and processed and made into things like automobiles. These vehicles had to be designed and built by those with intelligence (unless perhaps you're talking about the creators of the Yugo). I think you'd have to agree that an automobile, with its thousands of parts and all of its complexity, could never come together by itself no matter how many years go by. That would be like taking various metals, plastics, rubber, and other assorted materials, throwing them up in the sky, and expecting that millions or billions of years later they will come together as a well-equipped, fully-functional automobile. That's just not going to happen.

Actually, just the opposite is true. Once a complex vehicle is built, it isn't long before the process of decay begins. I have always been one who hand waxes my vehicles twice a year. It really does make them look good longer. But no matter how well I take care of them, eventually a rust spot will rear its ugly head. After a number of years, that same vehicle that may have been worth tens of thousands of dollars brand new will end up decaying in the junk yard. And that's the way it is with all things. Nothing left to itself ever gets better. Everything without the intervention of an intelligent designer eventually breaks down and decays. Things simply do not take on more order and complexity over the course of time as evolutionists would claim.

It is understandable that those who do not believe in God, or do not want to believe there is a God, would try to come up with theories to explain how everything began. Even as a Christian, it is impossible for me to wrap my finite mind around the fact that God has always existed and never had a beginning. I don't know if you're anything like me, but when I start thinking about where God came from, it's as if my mind begins to put up a "DOES NOT COMPUTE" message. I can almost see the sparks flashing in my cranium and the smoke starting to billow up.

It's just incomprehensible for us as human beings to imagine something or someone that never had a beginning. So those who do not accept the reality of God have to come up with theories such as the big bang to...uh..."create" their own explanations for how all things began.

There are, however, a couple of inescapable questions that are left unanswered by the Big Bang Theory. It is presented as an *origin* theory. But where did the primordial soup come from? And where did the energy come from that brought the universe to life? In reality, these "original" forms of matter absolutely had to have a beginning of their own. When you consider these questions it becomes apparent that the Big Bang Theory would still need a creator in order to work. In fact, the deeper you look into any origin theory the more plausible the Bible's account of creation becomes.

A COVER TO COVER REALITY

Once the literal truth of creation as presented in the Bible is established, then it is much easier to accept the reliability of the rest of Scripture. Even the more unbelievable historical accounts such as Noah and the ark or Jonah and the whale (or more correctly translated "the big fish") are suddenly understood to be entirely possible.

I worked as a sheriff's dispatcher for eight years in the 1990's and had occasional encounters with co-workers who were skeptical, and even antagonistic at times, about my Christian beliefs. One deputy in particular who was a good friend but wanted nothing to do with my faith would regularly chide me with questions like, "So tell me Randy, how did those animals get on the ark?" His implication was that it would be impossible for Noah to gather pairs of all the animals throughout the earth and get them onto the ark before the rains fell.

The truth is, it really *would* be impossible for Noah or anyone else to accomplish such a feat. (I have a hard enough time rounding up my two cats and getting them into the car when it's time to go to the vet!) But when you remember that all God had to do was speak a few words and everything we see was created, then getting all of the necessary animals into the ark — and later returning them to repopulate lands throughout the earth — is understood to be more than possible. God is not in any way constrained by human limitations. He can do anything, and this was clearly a supernatural act.

I have heard well-meaning Christians try to explain how other incredible things such as the parting of the Red Sea, or Jonah surviving in the belly of a large fish for three days, could have occurred in natural terms. For example, scientist Dr. Doron Nof, a professor of physical oceanography, created an experiment in 1992 in which he set up a model of the Red Sea to show how the Hebrew slaves could have escaped their former Egyptian owners as described in Exodus 14.

On the model's sea bottom he put a ridge and set up a fan that would blow the water. When he turned on the fan to replicate the "strong east wind" as mentioned in verse 21, the water separated, creating a dry area over the ridge. This theoretically would have provided a place for the Hebrews to pass through. (Further details of the experiment can be found at www.doronnof.net.)

This was hailed by many as a remarkable discovery proving that the biblical account of the Red Sea crossing could really have happened. But while I appreciate Dr. Nof's attempt to prove the accuracy of the Bible, I believe the experiment provided an unnecessary — and unlikely — explanation of the event.

The main reason for my skepticism is the fact that the two million or so Hebrews who crossed the Red Sea were not just strong, healthy adults, but also young children, the frail, and the elderly. If the wind was strong enough to blow the waters off the ridge, then I submit it would have been too overpowering for most, if not all of them, to walk through. They likely would have been blown right out of the sea.

The experiment indicated to me that even someone as brilliant Dr. Nof can focus too much on the natural in an attempt to prove the impossible. I believe a more likely explanation would be supernatural intervention. Those with Bible knowledge know that the crossing of the Red Sea became necessary when the Hebrews were leaving Egypt during the Exodus. Pharaoh had allowed the Jewish slaves to go free after his country experienced ten horrible plagues. Shortly after they had left, Pharaoh had a change of heart and ordered his troops to chase after the Hebrews and bring them back.

The former slaves ended up cornered at the edge of the Red Sea with no apparent escape route. While this may have seemed like a tactical error on the part of their leader Moses, the fact of the matter is they were led there by God with a pillar of cloud before them by day and a pillar of fire before them by night. God revealed in Exodus 14:4 that this was done so the Egyptians could see that He was the one, true Lord.

So this whole historical account is full of supernatural intervention on the part of God. The plagues thrust upon Egypt to gain the release of the Hebrew slaves, and the cloud and fire pillars, were obviously beyond the natural. So ultimately, I believe the parting of the Red Sea was just as supernatural. When you accept the truth about the eternal existence and all-powerful nature of God, then these types of "impossible" things are not just understood to be possible, but actually, likely. And really, no further explanation is necessary.

CULTURAL CONFUSION

Cultural differences between the Hebrews of the biblical era and we westerners of modern times can also create some confusion when distinguishing between what is literal in the Bible and what is literary. For example, it was common practice among the Jewish people to use hyperbole, or exaggeration, to make a critical point. It was not embellishment used as a way of manipulating the truth, but rather, an obvious exaggeration so the importance of the point wouldn't be missed. Take for instance the words of Jesus in Matthew 5:29-30:

> If your right eye causes you to sin, gouge it out and throw it away. It is better for you to lose one part of your body than for your whole body to be thrown into hell. And so if your right hand causes you to sin, cut it off and throw it away. It is better for you to lose one part of your body than for your whole body to go into hell.

It should be obvious that Jesus doesn't want us to literally pluck our eyes out if we struggle with lust, or chop off our hands if they have been used to fulfill sinful desires. If that were the case, there would be very few (if any) Christians out there walking around with both eyes and both hands. In fact,

if you were, say, walking around a shopping mall you would probably be able to distinguish who the Christians were because they would be the ones missing an eye, a hand, or both.

No, Jesus was just using the common Hebrew practice of exaggeration to make a critical point – that hell is a place you definitely want to avoid. (By the way, I defend the existence of a literal hell in the next chapter. Still, these verses make a tremendous case in and of themselves.) Similarly, Jesus said to the twelve disciples in Matthew 19:23-24:

> I tell you the truth, it is hard for a rich man to enter the kingdom of heaven. Again I tell you, it is easier for a camel to go through the eye of a needle than for a rich man to enter the kingdom of God.

If this were taken literally as we westerners would understand it, there would be absolutely no wealthy people in heaven because no camel could fit through the eye of a needle. But when understanding the Jewish way, Jesus was using obvious hyperbole to say wealth can be a tremendous stumbling block to salvation. In context with the whole passage, we can see that money often becomes an idol, and it can hinder the ability of rich people to see their need for God and His salvation. So Jesus exaggerates the point because He is not willing that any should perish, including the wealthy.

One final example I'll share can be found in the words of Jesus in Matthew 17:20:

> ...I tell you the truth, if you have faith as small as a mustard seed, you can say to this mountain, "Move from here to there" and it will move. Nothing will be impossible for you.

And again in Matthew 21:21:

> I tell you the truth, if you have faith and do not doubt... you can say to this mountain, "Go throw yourself into the sea," and it will be done.

Now clearly, Jesus is not saying we can literally move mountains and have them thrown into the sea. Common sense would tell us that mountains would be flying around all over the world if the smallest amount of faith could actually move them. Rather, the "mountain mover" analogy is an obvious exaggeration used to emphasize the point that the impossible is made possible through God.

WATCHING THE MOUNTAINS MOVE

One example of this truth would be in the giving of tithes. The most common understanding among Bible scholars today and throughout history is that tithing is the giving of one-tenth of our income to the church home where we are spiritually fed. After this firstfruit is brought to the "house of the Lord" (Exodus 23:19), then we can give what are called offerings that advance God's Kingdom in different ways — through missionaries or various other ministries.

If you have been a Christian for any length of time, you undoubtedly have heard from others — or experienced yourself — how the remaining 90 percent of income or less miraculously seems to go farther than the 100 percent would have gone. As a personal example, I have seen God save me thousands of dollars just through quirky mistakes when I am purchasing cars.

Several years ago there was a sweet 1996 Dodge Avenger for sale at a local one-man used car dealership. I needed a car and that model had been one of my favorites ever since it hit the market. But the price tag of $4,299 was a little rich for my pocketbook. Day after day as I drove to work I saw that Avenger and finally decided to give it a test drive. I was impressed and really wanted to buy it, but the owner of the lot couldn't come down in price as far as I needed him to go.

Then one day as I drove past, I noticed the price in the window had been dropped to $2,999. That I could handle! I stopped in and bought the car. When I asked him what happened, he said he wasn't making any money selling used cars so he was the quitting business by unloading his inventory at cost.

About four years later, our minivan had been totaled in an accident and we were looking to buy another. My wife spotted one that appeared to me to be way too expensive. The salesman told us it was priced at $6,100. We came back later to give it a test drive but he was gone, so a different salesman rode with us. He mentioned the price to be $6,999. What! We told him we couldn't come close to that and mentioned the price the other salesman had quoted. He said the other salesman had made a mistake but then added, "OK, then we'll start from there." To make a long story short, we ended up getting that van for about $5,250.

Another five years after that, we bought a different van which had been priced at $6,999 for only $5,000 because the price had been incorrectly entered into the dealership's web page at $5,999. Now believe me, I'm no genius negotiator. Yet in all, we ended up getting these three vehicles for some $5,000 dollars less than the asking price because of various unusual circumstances. Perhaps if it happened once you could make a case that it was a coincidence. But time after time after time? It sounds like supernatural provision to me. As it says it Malachi 3:10:

> Bring the whole tithe into the storehouse, that there may be food in my house. "Test me in this," says the Lord Almighty, "and see if I will not throw open the floodgates of heaven and pour out so much blessing that there will not be enough to store it."

I could also go on and on about the impossible made possible by God in relation to the many physical healings I've heard about and seen. In my own home, my wife had been battling clinical depression for many years that had required the use of medication. She went to a Christian women's conference one weekend, and for the next several days after returning home she would say, "How am I doing?"

That was a question she would ask from time to time when she wanted my assessment about her condition.

I was curious as to why she kept asking on a daily basis, but my reply each time was, "You're doing fine." It wasn't until several weeks later that she told me she had been prayed for at the women's conference and that she had been healed of her depression. That was many years ago now and she hasn't had to take medication since!

More recently, I had to have shoulder surgery because of a torn rotator cuff received playing football. It was an annual game on Thanksgiving morning that I had played with my brothers and several friends for some twenty-five years. The year following my surgery — despite the wise advice of my wife, daughters, parents, boss and others — I played again. And wouldn't you know it? I went down writhing in pain with a torn rotator cuff on the other shoulder.

This was a far more serious situation than the previous year. I wasn't looking forward to going through the surgery and months of physical therapy again for one thing. But apart from that, we had almost no money in our health savings account because of the injury the previous year. So the $2,500 deductible would have had to come out of pocket — and we didn't have it.

For several days, I prayed fervently to God for a miraculous healing. In all honesty, I had my doubts that it would actually happen. But I did have at least that mustard seed of faith, and little by little my shoulder started showing improvement. Praise the Lord! I knew my prayers were being answered because the other shoulder never improved, but only deteriorated until the surgery.

By the way, this testimony and my wife's healing from depression are also examples of God making the 90 percent go further when you tithe. In addition to saving the money on the deductible, we also have saved who knows how many hundreds, if not thousands, of dollars on the unneeded depression medications over the years.

Yes, God is a "Mountain Mover," regularly making the impossible, possible. So if you're waiting for answers to prayers such as these, don't give up because God is still in the miracle business! But keep in mind, whether His answer is yes, no, or wait a while, you can know that He is working all things together for your good and you can trust in Him (Romans 8:28).

LITERALLY LITERARY

Another potential point of confusion when confronting the question of the Bible as literal or literary has to do with the fact that some portions are actually symbolic or poetic. But this shouldn't be a stumbling block because when this is the case, we are actually clued into this fact. For instance, Jesus told forty parables — or stories — to help draw word pictures for his audience. It was a very effective method of helping people understand biblical truth, even though they were just fictional stories. The parables are found throughout the gospels of Matthew, Mark and Luke. And it is very clear that they are just that, fictional stories.

Unless it is obvious that the passage is symbolic, it should be taken literally. As an example, following a number of parables in the early part of Matthew, Jesus is asked by His disciples in Matthew 24 about what will happen at "the end of the age." There is no indication His answer is meant as a parable, analogy, or anything else. So when he says, for instance, in verse 11 that "many false prophets will appear and deceive many people" it should be understood to be literal.

Speaking of "the end of the age," the book of Revelation is probably the place where it is hardest to distinguish between a literal or literary interpretation. This is because virtually the whole book from Revelation 1:10 on is John's interpretation of a vision he received while "in the Spirit" on "the Lord's Day."

A significant amount of symbolic language is used, but unless otherwise noted, it should be taken literally. There is a great deal written about stars, scrolls, lions, lambs, beasts, dragons, etc. in the book of Revelation. While these are clearly symbolic images, they are used to represent literal people, places and events that will be a part of the last days — during the time of the Tribulation in particular. For example, the beast represents the Antichrist, and Satan is metaphorically presented as "the great dragon." This type of symbolism might be best understood by comparing it to a more recent example from C.S. Lewis' classic book *The Lion, the Witch, and the Wardrobe*.[7] The Lion is used to represent Jesus Christ, and the witch is a representation of satanic evil.

LITERARILY LITERAL

There are certain portions of Revelation that I believe can be moved without much effort from literary to literal in their meaning. Keep in mind John is writing, as best he can, what he is seeing in a prophetic vision. So he is likely trying to describe some very modern things with his ancient understanding.

Let's pretend for a moment that you are writing during the time of John and see a car in a vision, even though they wouldn't be invented for another eighteen hundred years or so. You might say something like, "and I saw before me a shiny horse with clear eyes that surrounded its head. It had a large nose that glowed at night and legs of black that were stationary but appeared to rotate." Of course, the shiny horse is the car, its clear eyes are the windows, the nose that glowed is the hood with its headlights, and the legs of black are the tires.

Admittedly, this is kind of a silly example but I hope it helps illustrate the point. John often made comments such as, "I saw something like..." or "I saw what looked like..." For instance, in Revelation 8 John is describing devastation that could be the result of a Tribulation period nuclear explosion, as a third of the earth is basically destroyed.

Similarly, in chapter 9 John's description of locusts coming out of a smoke-darkened sky could very well be an attempt to describe modern warplanes or military helicopters. After all, in the first century when John was writing there was no machinery or anything man-made that could fly so he was simply doing his best to interpret what he is seeing in his vision. The bottom line is that even with all of the symbolism found in Revelation, it should be understood — along with the entirety of the Bible — to be literal in its meaning unless we are clearly told otherwise.

CONCLUDING THOUGHT

The belief that the Bible can't be considered literal truth from God is invading the Kingdom at the highest levels. Even an early twenty-first century leader of the Catholic Church, Pope Benedict, said the Bible shouldn't be considered absolute authority from God. In September of 2008, Benedict addressed academics at the College des Bernardins in Paris. As reported in the *Catholic News Service,* he criticized the fundamentalist practice of interpreting the Bible literally saying, "the word of God can never simply be equated with the letter of the text." He added that, "at the beginning of all things, there must not be irrationality, but creative reason." This is a man who at the time was the spiritual leader of about 1.2 billion people in the world.

So Satan's first deception, "Did God really say...?" is alive and well today. And we're seeing the devastating impact in our modern churches — the results of which will be addressed, in part, in the chapters to come.

3–AN INCONVENIENT TRUTH: HELL

Most of us as Christians today are living our lives joyfully knowing our eternity is safe in the Lord. But very near to each one of us are people who are in great danger of hell fire. Yet we continue on as if nothing is wrong. Could this be, at least in part, a result of the growing indifference to the reality of hell?

Almost everyone would be aware that the title found in the next two chapters is a clever [author's commentary] take-off on Al Gore's 2006 documentary on global warming. In it, the former vice-president makes his case that the earth's atmosphere has been unnaturally warming in recent years and that man-made causes are responsible. Mr. Gore has been very passionate about this issue. He claimed in the documentary that the arctic ice has been melting at an alarming rate which ultimately will lead to coastal flooding throughout the world as the oceans rise. He also pointed to a very intense hurricane season in 2005 as evidence of dramatic climate change. That included Hurricane Katrina, the worst natural disaster to strike the United States up to that time.

AN INCOMPATIBLE TRUTH?

Gore said the solution lies largely in ridding the planet of vehicles and electric plants that are powered by so-called fossil fuels such as gas and coal, and replacing them with renewable energy sources such as wind and bio-fuels. This would minimize the production of carbon dioxide which is being called a greenhouse gas because of its perceived role in causing a warming of the atmosphere. He also said that human population control would be prudent.

Gore claimed that virtually every respected scientist and meteorologist is on board with the belief that man-made global warming is a real phenomenon and we must act now to save the planet. But I have heard from many who are also highly respected who say, "Not so fast." They make the case that any perceived warming in the earth's atmosphere in recent years is merely cyclical and something that has been observed in the past.

As an example, they point to the United States in the 1930's when many temperature records were set and still stand. It was so dry and hot in the central plains states that these were dubbed the nation's "dust bowl" years. This of course was well before millions of cars filled the highways and coal-fired power plants popped up across the world. Oddly enough, it was not all that long ago in the 1970's that some were fearing a new ice age was coming because of a prolonged period of below normal temperatures.

What do I believe about all of this? It might surprise you to find out that I really don't have a strong opinion. People that I respect are on both sides of the issue. However, I do have some skepticism because the belief in global warming has been used to advance political, financial, and other agendas.

One of these "other" agendas is strongly driven by a humanistic belief that God is not in control and that the human race is responsible for its own destiny. Let's face it, if you're convinced the fuels such as gas and coal that are used to power your car and heat and cool your home will eventually destroy the earth, you would likely join the chorus of people saying we need to change our energy focus. Add to that the fear some people have that these sources of fuel will one day run out, and you come to the conclusion that we must shift to completely renewable fuel sources.

But as a Christian, I believe that God has provided us with enough inexpensive sources of energy such as coal, crude oil, and natural gas to last for as long as we will need them. According to 1 Thessalonians 4:16-17, the day will come when Jesus returns to earth to take those who believe in Him to a heavenly home and the source of the energy we use will be a moot point. For what it's worth, I am also among the growing number of people who believe that crude oil is actually a renewable resource, being produced all the time through natural processes deep within the earth.

I don't want to be misunderstood. I believe we should do what we can to protect our environment and take care of this temporary residence God has provided for us, but I don't believe that should be done at the expense of the world's poor. They would be the ones most hurt by an abrupt shift away from the cheapest sources of energy. We should care about the environment, absolutely. But we should care about people more.

My skepticism is also driven by other factors. As I mentioned earlier, Gore pointed to an intense hurricane season in 2005 as evidence of global warming. However, in the years that followed the hurricane seasons were relatively mild. And as I'm writing today, there is a story in the news about a research vessel that has been stuck in ice near Antarctica for more than a week. Two icebreakers sent to rescue the ship have not been able to get through because of ice sheets that are up to 15 feet deep. Ironically, the trapped vessel went there to gather evidence of the impact of global warming. (If I was texting, this would have been a good time for an LOL.)

In addition, the temperature tonight outside of my Minnesota home is 16 below zero with an expected overnight low of 25 to 30 below. Record cold is in the forecast for the coming week, and temperatures here have been below normal almost the entire winter so far. (A little global warming is starting to sound pretty good right about now!)

Beyond any political or financial ambitions, I also believe there are well-meaning people who are sounding this alarm because of a true concern for the future. They are believing the predictions of increased drought, famine, and disease along with more frequent and stronger storms, wildfires, and even earthquakes. But again, we need to remember that God is in control. Ultimately, I believe that if global warming is real it will be used to fulfill biblical prophecy. Each of these predicted consequences can be found in Scripture as possible end times phenomena.

Could it be that the drought mentioned in Isaiah 24:4 is caused by global warming? With the worldwide commerce of the twenty-first century and a global population now topping seven billion you can imagine how a 1930's-type drought in the central plains states, the world's breadbasket, would impact widespread famine.

People like Mr. Gore say that increased carbon dioxide is making the oceans more acidic which is affecting the entire aquatic food chain. Could this lead to fulfillment of the prophecy in Revelation 16:3 which says that every living thing in the sea died? Can you imagine the impact on island and coastal countries that get most of their food and income from the ocean? Devastating famine would of course be a logical result.

Could the pestilence mentioned in Luke 21:11 be caused in part by longer warm weather seasons which help disease-carrying insects thrive and advance into new areas?

Could it be that the prophecy in Isaiah 24:17-20 which talks about opened floodgates in the heavens and the foundations of the earth being shaken is referring to the more frequent and stronger storms and earthquakes that are being blamed on global warming?

Could the billows of smoke and darkened sun in Joel 2:30-31 be a reference to the alleged increase in wildfires in recent years, and that are only expected to get worse, because of global warming?

No one knows the answers to these questions for sure, but I wouldn't doubt it if they were all "yes."

God often uses natural phenomena to bring about the fulfillment of His purposes and plans.

A TRASHY STORY ABOUT HELL

While the validity of global warming remains in doubt, there is one inconvenient truth we can be certain about — the existence of hell. I've just shared several passages of prophetic Scripture that could be fulfilled through the effects of global warming, but these are just the tip of the iceberg (pardon the expression) when you compare them to the number of references in the Bible to a real place called hell. As I alluded to, the aforementioned prophetic passages leave some room for conjecture. But the Scriptures relating to hell leave no doubt whatsoever that it does exist. That is unless you work very hard to create an alternate meaning.

Unfortunately, this is what has happened in increasing measure in recent years. Many people, including some very prominent and influential Christian leaders, have come out with explanations for what hell is or isn't that either have nothing to do with the Bible, or are an interpretation of Scripture that requires a significant stretch of the imagination to become reality.

For example, I was talking to a young man recently who was questioning the existence of a literal, eternal hell. He made reference to a teaching he heard from a well-known Christian leader saying that hell was actually, metaphorically speaking, a garbage dump that never stopped burning outside of Jerusalem. This teaching is based on several passages of Scripture, including Jeremiah 7:31-32:

> They have built the high places of Topheth in the Valley of Ben Hinnom to burn their sons and daughters in the fire — something I did not command, nor did it enter my mind. So beware, the days are coming, declares the Lord, when people will no longer call it Topheth or the Valley of Ben Hinnom, but the Valley of Slaughters, for they will bury the dead in Topheth until there is no more room.

Whether or not a trash dump actually existed at this site is a source of disagreement, but it was without question a horrible place. Some of the worst sins in Jewish history were committed in the valley mentioned here. It was used by the Jews as a place to worship idols and sacrifice their children by fire, similar to the practices of the Baal worshipers.

The name Valley of Ben Hinnom was translated from the Old Testament Hebrew word "ge'hinnom." And that word correlates with the New Testament Greek word "gehenna." Because of the evil that took place at this valley, gehenna as translated was used originally as a metaphor by the Jewish rabbis to describe punishment after death. So the implication in this "gehenna-as-a-trash-dump" teaching is that the biblical passages relating to hell are merely symbolic, referring to a self-imposed existence of temporary judgment and consequences on earth if we choose to live in disobedience to God.

However, this belief doesn't take into account that the concept of ge'hinnom or gehenna was used so often as a synonym for hell that it was later understood during the time of Jesus to mean hell itself, and was translated as such in the New Testament manuscripts. A further look at the original Greek in Matthew 10:28 adds verification to this assertion. Jesus said: "Do not be afraid of those who kill the body but cannot kill the soul. Rather, be afraid of the One who can destroy both soul and body in hell."

In this passage, the Greek word "apolesai" is added to gehenna. Apolesai means "delivered up to eternal misery." This should leave no doubt that the meaning of the word hell, as translated, is describing a literal, everlasting place of punishment after death.

A TRUE INCONVENIENT TRUTH

The previously mentioned passage from Jeremiah is used to explain away hell as something other than a literal place; it is someone's interpretation of Scripture. So what does the Bible really say about hell? Is it just a state of mind or a temporal consequence experienced by those who choose not to follow Jesus

Christ? Or is it a real place that will be an eternal home of suffering for those who reject Him? The Bible is actually chockfull of references to hell, so if we examine just a few of them we should certainly find the answers to these questions.

As a child growing up in a Christian home, things seemed very black and white to me. Those who accepted Jesus as their personal Savior and Lord went to heaven for eternity after they died. Those who chose to reject Him while on this earth would go to a place of eternal torment called hell. So naturally, the decision to accept Christ was easy for me and I assumed most people would want to do the same.

But as I grew older, I came to the realization that most people have not grasped that simple truth. As Matthew 17:13-14 says:

> Enter through the narrow gate. For wide is the gate and broad is the road that leads to destruction, and many enter through it. But small is the gate and narrow the road that leads to life, and only few find it.

One person I talked to about these verses asked me: "If most people go to hell, doesn't that mean that God loses and Satan wins?" And I must admit this was one of the tougher questions relating to this topic that I had to answer; not just for this individual, but for myself as well. It is an important question to be sure. Because if the answer is "yes" then it feeds doubt about what the Bible says, not just about hell, but about the very sovereignty of God. For if He is truly all-powerful, how could it be that most of the people He creates and loves end up spending an eternity in hell?

This is a reasonable question, and whole books have been written in an attempt to answer it with appropriate theology. But I am going to try to condense this complicated issue into the briefest, and hopefully the most understandable, of nutshells.

FREE WILL AND THE FREE GIFT

First of all, we have to keep in mind that the attributes of God cannot and will not change. He is the same yesterday, today, and forever (Hebrews 13:8). God created mankind with a free will so that each person could make their own choice whether or not to love Him and live for Him. The Holy Spirit convicts people of their sin and draws them to belief in God, but He is a gentleman. He will not force anyone to accept Jesus as their Savior.

But since the consequences of not accepting this free gift from God are so grave and eternal, wouldn't He want to...uh..."break the rules" to make sure we all spend eternity with Him someday? Whenever I am confronted with these types of tough questions relating to my heavenly Father, it is helpful when I think about my daughters' relationship with me, their earthly father.

Let's say one of my two adult daughters is choosing to live a life of rebellion. Just like God, I can give her all sorts of wise counsel and I can punish her when she disobeys. I can allow consequences to come into her life so she might see the wisdom in obeying me. I can do everything in my power to convince her to do what is right for her own good. But you know what? Because she has a free will, no matter how much I love her, my daughter can ultimately make the choice whether to submit to my authority or not. In the end, there is nothing I can do about it based on the limited level of control I have over her life. Similarly, by His own design, God cannot force her to be obedient. He has put a self-imposed limit on His authority based on the free will He has given her.

Why wouldn't God override a person's self-destructive choice to reject His love? An analogy that has to do with romantic relationships has helped put this question into perspective for me. If you are single, would you want to date someone who really wants nothing to do with you and has been forced to be with you against their will? Of course not. That would be a miserably discouraging relationship. Or would you rather spend your time with someone who really cares about you and wants to get to know you better?

Absolutely, because that would create an ongoing relationship of discovery and contentment.

If you are married, would you want to have a spouse who never wanted to marry you but was forced into the relationship? No way, for that would likely be among the most unhappy of marriages. Or would you rather have a spouse who chose you because they love and cherish you? Certainly, because that would create an ever-strengthening bond between two fulfilled people who could withstand any trial.

You see, God only wants to spend eternity with those who truly want to be with Him. The biblical relationship between the bride (the Church) and the Groom (Jesus) is just such a marriage. They love and cherish each other in a contented bond that can overcome anything they face. On an individual level, that is the kind of person with whom God wants to share His heavenly home — someone who loves and cherishes Him in the same way He loves and cherishes them.

God has already had to deal with a rebellion in heaven by created beings that did not want to want to submit to His authority. (We'll explore this more fully in the next chapter on Satan.) Could this be, at least in part, why God will steadfastly refuse to allow disobedient and unrepentant people into heaven? Instead, they will end up in the same place as Satan and his demons someday (Revelation 20:10-15) — but it is all by their own free will. God has provided a way of salvation through Jesus Christ. All they have to do is choose to surrender to Him and accept that free gift.

DISPUTED FREE WILL

There has been a teaching around for several centuries saying that God has already determined who will go to heaven and hell so our free will does not enter into the equation. It's part of a theology called *Calvinism* because it was developed by a priest named John Calvin who lived during the Protestant Reformation. He based his theology of pre-determinism on several verses relating to election and predestination. For example, in Romans 8:29-33 Paul wrote:

For those God foreknew He also predestined to be con-
formed to the likeness of His Son, that He might be the
firstborn among many brothers. And those He predestined,
He also called; those He called, He also justified; those He
justified, He also glorified.

And again in Ephesians 1:4-5:

For He chose us in Him before creation of the world to be
holy and blameless in His sight. In love he predestined us
to be adopted as His sons through Jesus Christ, in accor-
dance with His pleasure and will...

The "called" and those God chose are the elect. Several verses
bear this out. Among them is Matthew 24:31 which talks about
the second coming of Christ:

And He will send His angels with a loud trumpet call, and
they will gather His elect from the four winds, from one
end of the heavens to the other.

So the way Calvin interpreted these passages, before we were
even born God alone made the choice as to who would be the
elect and they were exclusively predestined to be His children
now and for eternity. As Calvin wrote in his 1536 seminal work,
Institutes of the Christian Religion, "All are not created on equal
terms, but some are preordained to eternal life, others to eternal
damnation; and, accordingly, as each has been created for one or
other of these ends, we say that he has been predestined to life
or to death."

Though he lived about five hundred years ago, the influence
of some of Calvin's theology is still felt today. His teaching is
fine if you are among the predestined elect. But what if you're
not? What if you believe you, or someone you love, is on the
outside looking in? What if you believe your eternal destiny, or
the eternal destiny of a loved one, could be hell? It is not hard to
see why such a theology would cause someone to try to reinterpret what the Bible says. After all, if God is just and loving, He

certainly wouldn't send anyone to an eternal place of torment without giving them any say in the matter.

Since God is not willing that any should perish (2 Peter 3:9), I too believe that He would never allow anyone to go to such a horrible place without sovereign justification. But rather than change what the Bible says about hell, maybe we need to reevaluate what is commonly believed about Calvin's teaching on election and predestination. I know that I am dealing with a thorny theological issue here, but please bear with me as I make my case. I mean no disrespect to Calvin or his followers. But whether correctly understood or not, I believe Calvinistic teachings have led to spiritual detriment for many people over the years.

In 2 Peter 1:10-11, one of Jesus' closest disciples gives us a key perspective on what being the elect is truly all about:

> Therefore, my brothers, be all the more eager to make your calling and election sure. For if you do these things, you will never fall, and you will receive a rich welcome into the eternal kingdom of our Lord and Savior Jesus Christ.

In these verses it appears quite clear that election is our responsibility. *We* are told to make our calling and election sure. When Peter says "if you do these things" he is referring to *our* choice to grow in maturity as Christians. In context with the previous verses 5 through 9, and really with the rest of the Bible, it's evident that we become the elect when we choose to accept Jesus as our Savior and establish Him as Lord by making every effort to glorify Him with our lives. When we become among the elect by our own choice, we are then "glorified" (Romans 8:30) and predestined for an eternity spent with God.

I'd like to share an analogy that hopefully will provide some clarity on the issue:

> There is a lush valley surrounded by a forest, and a multitude of people residing in the valley. Unbeknownst to most of them, a wildfire is burning in the forest and it is moving ever closer. Along the only road through the valley comes

a bus named "Predestination" and its driver is Jesus. He stops, warns the people of the approaching fire, and invites them to come aboard so He can drive them to safety. Many join Him, but even more are having too much fun enjoying what the lush valley has to offer. Despite the numerous pleas from Jesus and the many who have joined Him on the bus, these people choose to ignore the danger posed by the fire while they continue to eat, drink, and be merry. Eventually, Jesus has to drive out of the valley on the only road that leads to safety. The people that accepted Jesus' invitation to join Him are saved, while the people who rejected Him eventually perish in the fire.

The point of the analogy is this: the "bus" is on a predestined journey to heaven. Those who choose to accept Jesus' invitation become the elect, and they are saved.

In other words, God did preordain that the elect would go to heaven. But in context with the rest of Scripture, it should be understood that *we* make the choice whether or not to become part of His elect. After all, if our eternal destination has already been decided by God, then significant amounts of the Bible would not be necessary. Why would there be any need for passages about the importance of believing, repenting, growing in our maturity as believers, dying to self and living for Christ, or being witnesses and missionaries for God?

No, free will puts the primary responsibility for where we will spend eternity on us. God draws us by His Holy Spirit and provides the tools we need to succeed as believers. But ultimately the choice is ours. And when we choose to surrender and make Jesus the "bus driver" of our lives, then we become among the elect who are predestined to make the journey to heaven with Him someday.

THE IMPLICATION OF AMPUTATIONS

As wonderful as this invitation sounds, there are many people I have come to care very deeply about that want nothing to do with this Savior who has become so precious to me. So I have begun to understand on a very personal level why it can become so attractive to change what we believe about hell. Still, I cannot get past what the Bible says about the issue when it is simply taken at face value. In 2 Thessalonians 1:7-9 it says:

> This will happen when the Lord Jesus is revealed from heaven in blazing fire with His powerful angels. He will punish those who do not obey the gospel of our Lord Jesus. They will be punished with everlasting destruction and shut out from the presence of the Lord and from the majesty of His power...

These are words penned by the Apostle Paul, but Jesus also spoke many times about hell as a real place. In the book of Matthew alone, Jesus talks about hell as a place "where there will be weeping and gnashing of teeth" in 8:12; 13:42, 50; 22:13; 24:51; and 25:30. And as I shared in the previous chapter, a couple of other verses emphasize the reality of hell and the seriousness Jesus placed on the issue — Matthew 5:29-30. But a similar passage makes an even stronger case. Matthew 18:8-9 says:

> If your hand or your foot causes you to sin, cut it off and throw it away. It is better for you to enter life maimed or crippled than to have two hands and two feet and be thrown into eternal fire. And if your eye causes you to sin, gouge it out and throw it away. It is better for you to enter life with one eye than to have two eyes and be thrown into the fire of hell.

As explained in the last chapter, Jesus is employing a common Hebrew practice here of using exaggeration to make a critical point — that hell is a place you absolutely do *not* want to be. But this passage brings even greater clarification — hell is a place of eternal fire. Add to that Jesus' description of hell as a place "where there will be weeping and gnashing of teeth," and Paul's words that the disobedient "will be punished with everlasting destruction." It soon becomes obvious that when you take the Word of God literally, hell is a real place of eternal torment.

SILENCING THE LAMBS

I don't want anyone I love or truly care about to end up in a place like this, do you? Of course not, nobody does. And therein lies the desire to change hell, if it exists at all, into something that is a milder, temporary punishment. But by doing this, I believe we are doing Satan a great favor. I tend to agree with what Brian Jones said in his compelling book, *Hell is Real: But I Hate to Admit It*:

> "Practically speaking, if everyone goes to heaven, why bother with Jesus at all? Why attend church? Why serve? Why tithe? Why share our faith with others (Great Commission)? None of this makes any sense. Why would we do anything beyond that which makes us feel good?... But if hell is real, it changes everything. I'm convinced that if we were to truly believe in hell, there would be no cost too high, no sacrifice too great, no pain too unbearable to keep us from doing everything in our power to convince people of this reality and show them the way out. To live any other way would be unthinkable."[8]

Before Jones wrote this, he said in his book that he had gone to seminary and had been a pastor for several years while keeping the secret that he didn't believe hell was a real place — for many of the same reasons mentioned in this chapter. But he had an encounter with God while on a sabbatical. Jones said the Lord confronted him about his lack of belief in hell, even though he did accept what the Bible said about everything else. This transformed his thinking, and with that, gave him an "apocalyptic urgency" to share the gospel with as many people as possible.

When we take hell out of the picture the urgency to share our faith becomes, for lack of a better word, optional. The Great Commission in Matthew 28:19, in which Jesus commands us to "go and make disciples of all nations," becomes a moot point — a totally unnecessary waste of time.

It reminds me of a time several years ago when I was at a special outdoor event at a local church organized by a youth ministry. It was a warm, sunny, summer day and people of all ages were having a wonderful time playing in the inflatable games and listening to several bands perform. Meanwhile, just a few miles down the road a wildfire was raging out of control. The homes, property, and very lives of many people were being endangered. As I watched fire trucks, ambulances, and police cars race past the church for much of the afternoon, the irony of the situation created an eye-opening spiritual analogy.

Most of us as Christians today are living our lives joyfully knowing our eternity is safe in the Lord. But very near to each one of us are people who are in great danger of hell fire. Yet we continue on as if nothing is wrong, going about our lives in blissful ignorance feeling secure in our eternity with God, but not too concerned about what eternity might hold for others.

Could this be, at least in part, a result of the growing indifference to the reality of hell? This is among the reasons I consider this to be a key Kingdom invader. I believe Satan is using a lack of belief in hell among Christians as an effective weapon to silence God's people.

A KINDER, GENTLER HELL

Oddly enough, the teachings of extra-biblical religions have likely contributed to the modern reevaluation of what hell really is. For instance, the Mormons teach that all people will enter one of three heavens when they die. The "bad" people must suffer for a while in hell before entering the lowest of the heavens. So Mormon doctrine says there is a hell, but it is merely a temporary place. It's kind of like going to jail until you have paid your debt to society, and then you are released.

Another religious group that contradicts what God's Word says about a real, eternal hell is the Seventh Day Adventists. Their belief is a little less complex. SDA's teach that people go into a "soul sleep" when they die. Only through Jesus Christ does a person put on immortality. So those who are saved according to the Scriptures as interpreted by SDA founder Ellen G. White (through a combination of works and grace) will awaken at the resurrection to eternal life. Those who are not saved as SDA's will simply remain in soul sleep forever; they will be annihilated and cease to exist. This belief is called nihilism, and it means there will be no everlasting torment and therefore no need for a hell.

When you read these explanations about what hell is or isn't, perhaps you felt it resonate with your own desire for a kinder, gentler eternal disposition for those who reject Christ. And I'm sure whoever came up with such theology really wanted to believe that it was true. But in the end, these beliefs are not backed by Scripture. As I've already stated, anything that we believe about anything is just opinion unless we compare it to the absolute truth contained in God's Word.

NO QUASI-EXPLANATIONS ALLOWED

Perhaps the clearest biblical proof that hell is a real place of eternal torment, as has always been taught in orthodox Christianity, is found in the words of Jesus in Luke 12:4-5:

> I tell you, my friends, do not be afraid of those who kill the body and after that can do no more. But I will show you whom you should fear: Fear him who, after the killing of the body, has power to throw you into hell. Yes, I tell you, fear him.

Jesus Himself said, "Fear him who, *after the killing of the body*, has the power to throw you into hell." This allows for no quasi-explanations of hell as a metaphorical garbage dump on earth, or earthly consequences we face for not being obedient to God. Hell is a real place that, after death, will be the destination for those who refuse to submit to God's authority (including His requirement that we believe in and accept Jesus His Son as our Savior).

By the way, any notion that a loving God would never send anyone to hell is refuted with these short but revealing verses. Jesus says it is not only acceptable, but wise, to have a healthy fear of the Lord. He even repeats Himself so that we won't miss the point. In understanding God's immeasurable love for us, it is more insightful to look at all that He has done to *rescue* us from hell. God has given us His instruction manual, the Bible, to tell us all we need to know in order to be saved, and has sent His very own Son, Jesus, to die on a cross as payment for our sins.

Would you be willing to allow your child to suffer and die if the choice was yours? Neither would I. But that's the kind of love God has for us. And this points to a crucial question that simply must be answered: If a real, eternal hell does not exist, then what did Jesus die to save us from?

THE SECOND DEATH

It would probably come as no surprise that the final biblical argument for an actual place of torment called hell can be found in the book of Revelation. Without going too deeply into end times theology, the Antichrist and false prophet who are used by Satan to wreak havoc during the Great Tribulation are thrown into the "fiery lake of burning sulfur" at the end of that seven year period (Revelation 19:19-20).

Satan himself is sealed up in an "abyss" during the ensuing Millennium. Then he is released one last time to try to convince children born during this thousand-year period to turn away from God. This happens because all people born at any time in history will have the same opportunity to either submit to God or reject Him. (Of course, God's merciful nature would assure that there are exceptions for those whose young age or mental capacity prevents their ability to make that choice.) Soon after, Satan is reunited with the Antichrist and false prophet as he too is cast into hell. As John writes in Revelation 20:10:

And the devil, who deceived them, was thrown into the lake of burning sulfur, where the beast [Antichrist] and the false prophet had been thrown. They will be tormented day and night forever and ever.

After that, there is what is called a Great White Throne Judgment in which those who have rejected God during their lives are thrown into the "lake of fire" along with Satan and his allies. This is called the "second death" in verse 14 because, like the physical-realm death to the body, it is a spiritual-realm death that lasts "day and night forever and ever."

HELL FOR THOSE WHO HAVEN'T HEARD?

I'd like to deal briefly with one final and very valid question about hell which has been asked throughout history: What about those in remote areas of the world who never heard about Jesus during their lifetimes? Would it be fair for God to send them to hell?

My answer will be brief only because I don't think a highly-intellectual response is necessary. As I touched on a moment ago in my comments about children born during the Millennium, the fact of the matter is that all people of accountable mind born at any time in history will have the same opportunity to either submit to God or reject Him. We can know this because it is His nature to be a God of perfect justice. The Lord chooses to work through His people, whether it be their prayers, finances, or missionary service. But when His servants aren't able to fulfill the mission in the natural, I truly believe God makes sure that everyone has the same blessed hope for salvation — even if it requires some form of supernatural intervention.

CONCLUDING THOUGHT

It is important that we don't make hell our focus when trying to get people saved, or as a way of scaring Christians into behaving righteously. But the topic should not be avoided either.

I once heard the proper teaching of hell described as ballast in a ship. Ballast doesn't steer the ship or give it guidance or direction, but it does provide balance to keep the vessel from being tossed about dangerously on the waves. Certainly we need to be taught regularly about the doctrines relating to God's unconditional love and immeasurable grace, but knowing the truth about hell provides a balance that keeps us from being dangerously tossed about by every wave of doctrine. It helps us in understanding that we do have a serious responsibility to live out our faith appropriately before the Lord.

There was a pastor who spoke at a recent family Bible camp I attended in which his message revolved around a shocking statement: "I wish everyone could go to hell." This obviously was an attention grabber. Then he went on to explain what he meant, and his point was very well taken. He said if everybody could go to hell and see what it was really like — with all of its loneliness, tears, and suffering — then each person would come away changed. The unsaved would want to accept Jesus as their Savior because they would not want to spend their eternity in hell. And those who are already saved would live their lives with a renewed sense of urgency, doing whatever they could make sure that no one they knew would end up there.

While a temporary visit is not a possibility, hopefully the many passages of Scripture I've shared in this chapter have given an insight into the reality of hell. And with this reality in mind, may we who are Christians strive to live in such a way that we reflect the love and righteousness of Christ. Our witness can make Jesus so irresistible that those we care about will desire to make their eternal home with Him in heaven — the amazing, glorious alternative that God has prepared for those who love Him.

4–AN INCONVENIENT TRUTH: SATAN

Satan is propagating the lie that he does not exist because he knows if you don't believe there is an enemy to battle, then you won't build your defenses, your guard will be down, and you won't be prepared to fight the spiritual battles when they come.

As I stated in chapter two, God is a spirit being who has always existed. On a time line of eternity, this earth and all that we see would consist of only a microscopic pin-prick in the middle of a God who always was and a future that will never end. Before the earthly pin-prick, God created other spirit realm beings — the angels — that dwelt with Him in heaven prior to what is recorded in Genesis 1.

There was a rebellion led by an angel named Lucifer in which he and one-third of the angels turned against God. They became the demons. They were subsequently cast out of heaven and eventually sent to the earth. This "prequel" to Genesis can be found in Revelation 12, where John sees a vision and describes the rebellion in heaven, the exile to earth, and the subsequent attempts by the powers of darkness to destroy God's chosen people, the Jews, and the grafted-in chosen, the Christians.

THE REALM REALITY

So Genesis is the account of the beginning of *physical* creation. With this important understanding we can now make sense of the serpent in the Garden of Eden who was trying to tempt Eve to sin. The physical-realm serpent had been indwelt by the spirit-realm Lucifer, known also as Satan or the devil. Because Eve and then Adam were deceived when asked the age old question "Did God really say...?" Satan succeeded in gaining the foothold he needed to begin wreaking havoc on God's creation for thousands of years to come. This is difficult to understand because our physical-realm minds have a hard time comprehending matters of the spirit realm. For clarification, let's just think of it in terms of how prayer works.

There was a Bible college president who was speaking at a summer camp I was attending one year and he mentioned an incident that had occurred just before camp began. He had been trying to sleep one night when he felt an overwhelming sense in his spirit that God wanted him to pray for a friend who was great distance away. He said he prayed for about fifteen minutes for what he knew, and then about fifteen minutes in the Spirit about what he couldn't know, before he felt a release and went back to bed.

The next day he called the friend to find out what, if anything, had happened that night. This person said he had faced a serious situation associated with some legal issues that were not his fault. This happened at the precise moment that the Holy Spirit prompted the one man to pray for the other.

It was very clear that the physical-realm prayers of this Bible college president had impacted the physical-realm world of his friend. In between, however, was a spirit-realm conduit that literally reached across many miles. What happened first in the physical-realm prayers, brought movement in the spirit realm, which impacted the physical-realm reality. No one saw what happened in the spirit realm during those prayers, but likely there was a multitude of angels dispatched to bring about an answer in keeping with the will of God.

This is similar to the supernatural change that occurs when we accept Jesus as our Savior and Lord. It is a simple act of our physical-realm wills that "invites" the spirit-realm Holy Spirit to dwell within us. That begins a transformation that impacts our physical-realm reality as the fruit of the Spirit becomes increasingly evident in our lives.

In the same way, a supernatural change occurred when Adam and Eve made that first choice to disobey God. It was a simple act of their physical-realm wills that "invited" the spirit-realm powers of darkness to dwell on the earth. This began a transformation that has allowed evil to impact the physical realm for several thousand years now, introducing the reality of pain, disease, suffering, and death to the world (Romans 5:12).

With that one sin, Adam and Eve unlocked a door that had prevented Satan from receiving the "permission" he needed to begin implementation of his devilish, hellish plans against God and His creation. Just like an intruder who plans to commit every kind of mischief once he gets into your home — to steal, kill, destroy, rape, pillage, and every other vile act against you and your family — so Satan entered the unlocked door when given the opportunity and has committed atrocities against God's physical creation ever since.

But just as the police eventually arrive to arrest the intruder, Satan will one day be "taken into custody." He will no longer be allowed to harm the occupants of the world and will ultimately face a Judge who will find Satan guilty on all counts. The Judge will have him locked in "prison" and the key will be thrown away for eternity.

THE SATAN REALITY

With all that being said, if you don't believe Satan exists then none of this matters whatsoever. But denying his existence means you have to discount a significant portion of the Bible as merely literary and not absolute truth from God. (I pray that the evidence presented in the first two chapters of this book will be enough to convince you that the infallibility of the Scriptures can be trusted.)

The late Christian singer Keith Green, who some considered to be a modern day prophet, became aware in the late 1970's of the increasing belief that Satan does not exist. So Green made a conscious attempt to include a song about Satan on each of his albums. On his 1977 debut album *For Him Who Has Ears to Hear* (Sparrow Records) that song was called, "No One Believes In Me Anymore." In it, I think Green hit the nail on the head when he implied that the devil is proudly working toward anonymity. As if speaking for Satan, Green penned these words:

> I used to have to sneak around
> But now they just open their doors
> You know, no one's watching for my tricks
> Because no one believes in me anymore.

Several decades ago, Green was already tuned into the fact that many Christians were beginning to believe Satan does not exist. And this thought has been invading the Kingdom in increasing measure ever since. Satan is propagating the lie because he knows that if you don't believe there is an enemy to battle, then you won't build your defenses, your guard will be down, and you won't be prepared to fight the spiritual battles when they come. But the Bible talks extensively about Lucifer, Satan, the devil — and not in allegorical terms. He is discussed as a real being that we must be concerned about, battle against, and overcome through the power of the Holy Spirit.

We already looked at the angel Lucifer, his rebellion in heaven, and his physical incarnation as a serpent in the Garden of Eden. But that is just the beginning of the Bible's discussion of the spirit-realm being who is called Satan after his expulsion from heaven. I use the term "being" because satanic evil is not just a force or the absence of good as some believe. Any serious study of Scripture reveals that Satan *is* a real being with evil intent against God and His creation.

The book of Job contains a remarkable "fly on the wall" look at the reality of Satan and his relationship with God. Satan wickedly chided God by saying Job was only a righteous servant because the hedge of protection placed around him had prevented him from facing any real hardship. To prove Satan wrong, God allowed him to inflict Job with all manner of trials and tribulations, including the loss of his possessions and livelihood, the death of his children, and the onset of painful sickness and disease.

While it is hard to understand why bad things happen to good people, there are some important lessons to be learned from the book of Job. First, Satan can only do to us as Christians what God allows him to do — we need not fear that Satan can crush us without restraint. Not only do we see this is Job 1:12, but also in Luke 22:31. Jesus is talking to His impulsive disciple Simon Peter when He says, "Simon, Simon. Satan has asked to sift you as wheat. But I have prayed for you, Simon, that your faith may not fail." Did you catch that? Satan had to ask for *permission* before he could do anything to Peter.

Second, the bad things we face — including sickness — are not always consequences for unwise or sinful choices. They can be, but often times we face trials because God has a higher purpose in allowing them — either for us or for His Kingdom. James 1:2 can at first glance seem among the most preposterous of verses in the whole Bible: "Consider it pure joy, my brothers, whenever you face trials of many kinds..." But James goes on in verses 3 and 4 to bring clarification to the statement: "...because you know that the testing of your faith develops perseverance. Perseverance must finish its work so that you may be mature and complete, not lacking anything."

This is similar to trees that grow in a windy area. Their roots go deeper into the soil so the tree can withstand virtually any storm that comes their way. So it is with those of us who are Christians. As we endure trials, and persevere in our faith, we become able to stand up to whatever storms come our way. So you can count on it — we as Christians will from time to time face difficulties that we don't understand. But rest assured, God is allowing them ultimately for our good and the good of the Kingdom.

Third, when we persevere and are faithful to God in the midst of our trials, we will be rewarded beyond our greatest expectations. In Job's case, he received earthly rewards double what he had before Satan's attacks. While we can't always expect that our rewards will come here on earth, we can be certain that our heavenly reward will be worth any price we paid in our faithfulness to God.

The Apostle Paul was a man who understood this. He was imprisoned and beaten multiple times for the sake of Christ, yet knew it would ultimately be worth it. He likened the Christian life to a race with a prize waiting at the end. In 1 Corinthians 9:24-25 he said:

> Do you not know that in a race all the runners run, but only one gets the prize? Run in such a way as to get the prize. Everyone who competes in the games goes into strict training. They do it to get a crown that will not last; but we do it to get a crown that will last forever.

One other lesson can be learned from the words of Jesus mentioned earlier in Luke 22:31. Understanding full well Satan's evil plans for Simon Peter, Jesus said that He had prayed for him. From this we can know that it is completely reasonable and wise to pray for protection from satanic attacks, whether they be temptations as in Peter's case, or physical attacks such as those faced by Job.

SATAN SCHEMES TO SCUTTLE SALVATION

In keeping with the purpose of this chapter, perhaps you have already noticed something very pertinent in the passage I just shared from the book of Luke — Jesus, the Son of God Himself, believes in Satan as a real being. We are once again given a "fly on the wall" look at a conversation, this time between Satan and

Jesus, in both Matthew 4 and Luke 4. Satan was in the process of doing what he does best. He met up with Jesus in the wilderness, trying to tempt Him to sin before His earthly ministry began.

Satan attacked Jesus in some of the same ways he goes after us; hoping to use pride, greed, and selfishness to entice Jesus into an act of iniquity. After all, Satan knew that if he could deceive Jesus into committing even one sin, then God's redemptive plan would have been null and void. Mankind would have been forever separated from a holy God who cannot dwell in the presence of any unrighteousness.

In the Old Testament, the blood of animals that had no blemish or defects had to be shed as a sacrifice for the sins of God's people. But this was only a temporary fix. The permanent solution came when Jesus was crucified on a cross. But for His sacrifice to mean anything, Jesus had to be seen as "a spotless lamb" without blemish or defects in the eyes of God. That meant He had to be righteous and pure — sinless — in and of Himself. Therefore, if Satan could have tempted Jesus to sin even once, you and I would have had no hope for salvation. Satan was fully aware of this when he tempted Jesus in the wilderness.

This is the heart of the Gospel, that the blood of Jesus was shed on a cross to wash away our sins. So those of us who believe in Jesus and His sacrifice are seen as righteous and pure in the eyes of God, worthy to spend eternity with Him in our heavenly home.

Jesus was about thirty years old at the time of the wilderness temptation. But way back when He was just a baby, Satan was already trying to do what he could to eliminate God's plan of salvation in a different way. When Jesus was about two years old, it is recorded in Matthew 2 that Satan used a jealous and paranoid King Herod in an attempt to kill Jesus. Herod heard about this baby who was born "King of the Jews" so he ordered the murder of all males born at about the same time as Jesus in the area of Bethlehem. But Jesus' earthly father, Joseph, was warned in a dream about Herod's evil plan and took his family to Egypt where the Savior would be safe. A proper understanding of spiritual warfare leaves no doubt that Satan was the driving force behind Herod's obsession to kill Jesus.

I believe a final attempt to prevent Jesus from fulfilling His divine purpose occurred in the hours before His crucifixion. When I saw the 2004 Mel Gibson movie *The Passion of the Christ* I came to the conclusion that Satan tried to kill Jesus just before He could make it to the cross. As I was watching the film, I cringed at the merciless abuse Jesus received. After His arrest, when Jesus appeared before the Jewish court, they spit on Him, and slapped and punched Him. When Jesus was turned over to the Roman soldiers they brutally whipped Him, mocked Him, put a crown of sharp thorns on His head, spit on Him, and repeatedly struck Him on the head with a stick.

As He was being led through the city of Jerusalem to the place where He would die, the soldiers had to force another man to carry Jesus' cross because He was so weak from the torture He had endured. Jesus had been so horribly abused that he may have been unrecognizable even to those closest to Him (Isaiah 52:14).

As I was watching the movie, I kept wondering why the Jewish religious leaders, the Roman soldiers, and many of the average citizens despised Jesus so much. Their hatred was just seething even though Jesus wasn't a thief, murderer, rapist, or any other type of criminal that usually prompts a vengeful response from victims.

And then it dawned on me. I began to think with a spirit-realm perspective and realized that if Jesus was brutalized to the point of death *before* He hung on the cross, then many of the prophecies related to His death would not have been fulfilled and His divine purpose would have been defeated. I believe Satan knew this, so he began planting seeds of hatred toward Jesus in any willing human vessel and the result became clear in the horrific treatment he endured before His death.

But Jesus did survive and died at the appointed place at the appointed time, and then rose to life again so that we could have the opportunity to join Him in a heavenly home someday. In the meantime, Satan will not give up. Even though Jesus is now safely in heaven at God's right hand, the Bible makes it clear that Satan will continue to attack God's chosen people, the Jews, and the grafted-in chosen, the Christians.

A HATED PEOPLE

Just as it makes no sense that Jesus was so hated before His crucifixion, it also makes no sense that the Jews have been so hated by so many people throughout history. The Jews that I have met have been very nice people, the kind you would like as your neighbors. I have only known them to be good citizens and hard workers. If you were in a store checkout line with a Jew, or if you were to sit next to one at a sporting event or concert, you likely wouldn't even know they were Jewish. So of all the people groups in the world — that have existed or still exist — why have the Jews been so hated and persecuted?

From their enslavement in Egypt some thirty-five hundred years ago, to their captivity in Assyria and Babylon more than twenty-five hundred years ago, to their oppression under Roman rule during the time of Jesus, to the barbaric holocaust at the hands of Nazi Germany during World War II, the Jewish people have faced unjust persecution throughout history. Even to this day they have hostile neighbors in the Middle East that want their homeland of Israel "wiped off the face of the earth" to quote the maniacal leader of one nearby country.

To understand the hatred toward the Jewish people, and now the nation of Israel, it is time once again to do some spirit-realm thinking. In Deuteronomy 7:6 the Jews were for the first time described as God's "chosen people." That automatically made them a target for Satan, who hates God and anyone He favors. So throughout history, Satan has found willing vessels to attack, oppress, and even kill the Jewish people such as in the examples above. It should also be pointed out that Jesus is a Jew. So if Satan could have wiped out the Jewish race before the crucifixion, this also would have been effective in defeating God's redemptive plan for humanity.

So mark my words, we will continue to see examples of anti-Semitism — or the hatred of Jews — until the Glorious Appearing of Jesus on the earth (Revelation 19:11-21). Until then, whenever you see reports of any person, nation, or religious group attacking the Jews or Israel — either verbally or with violence — keep in mind they are being used as willing vessels to carry out Satan's evil plans.

The influence of Satan is not limited of course to attacks on the Jewish people. He is also very active in trying to destroy the grafted in chosen, the Christians, as we are described in Romans 11:11-24. That is why we have to continually put on our protective spiritual armor. Paul references this spirit-realm battle in Ephesians 6:11-12:

> Put on the full armor of God so that you can take your
> stand against the devil's schemes. For our struggle is not
> against flesh and blood, but against the rulers, against
> the authorities, against the powers of this dark world and
> against the spiritual forces of evil in the heavenly realms.

In a nutshell, we put on our spiritual armor when we spend time with God every day in worship, prayer, and Bible study; and when we strive to live holy lives, making every effort to be obedient to God's commands. This spiritual discipline hinders Satan's ability to wreak havoc. It also gives us the enhanced ability to discern when evil thoughts and practices are invading the Kingdom of God.

THE CHOSEN VS. THE CHOSEN

By the way, just because we become grafted in "Jews" when we accept Jesus as our Savior doesn't mean we have replaced them as God's chosen people. There are many Christians who have come to accept what is called "replacement theology." This is a false teaching that basically says God has abandoned the Jews as His chosen people because of their continued rebellion toward Him and we should no longer consider them to be the apple of God's eye.

Replacement theology becomes completely dismantled, however, when you read in Deuteronomy 9:6-7 that God said His decision to choose the Jews in the first place had nothing to do with their obedience or lack thereof. In addition, there is an end times prophecy concerning the Jewish people in Revelation 7:1-8. There are 144 thousand Tribulation servants of God that are listed as descendants of the twelve tribes of Israel. Why would these Jews be specifically singled out unless they are of primary importance to the plan of God right to the very end? Still, replacement theology has led many people today to believe that any Bible-based support for the Jewish people and the nation of Israel is misplaced.

This is not the first time in history that some Christians have become hostile toward Jews. There was a belief circulating in the Middle Ages that the Jewish people were worthy of persecution and even death because they were responsible for the crucifixion of Jesus. This mindset went to the highest levels as even the great reformer himself, Martin Luther, was a proponent of such anti-Semitism.

It was a curious viewpoint because Jesus' crucifixion fulfilled crucial biblical prophecy and meant that we would have the opportunity for salvation. So if anything else, we should thank the Jews for providing both salvation and the sacrificial Lamb, because Jesus Himself was Jewish. By the way, it was technically the Roman soldiers — Gentiles, not Jews — that put Jesus on the cross and killed Him. And in the broader reality it was actually all of humanity, and our sin, that sent Jesus to the cross.

Ultimately, a spirit-realm perspective leads to the conclusion that these beliefs on the part of Christians have been additional satanic attempts to destroy the Jewish people. Because if all the peoples of the earth — including Christians — believe Jews are not worthy of favor, then they theoretically become vulnerable to extinction.

We must keep in mind what God told Abram (later Abraham), who was the first of the Hebrew or Jewish people, in Genesis 12:2-3:

> I will make you into a great nation and I will bless you; I will make your name great, and you will be a blessing. I will bless those who bless you, and whoever curses you I will curse; and all the peoples on earth will be blessed through you.

I believe this is why the United States became the world's most powerful and prosperous nation beginning in the second half of the twentieth century. It seems to be more than a coincidence that the ascension of the U.S. in world dominance came after Israel became a nation again in 1948. From the start, the U.S. has been a strong ally of Israel when the rest of the world has largely abandoned them. And I truly believe it is to our peril as a nation if we ever go from "blessing" them to "cursing" them.

Regardless, God will keep His hand on Israel come what may. Just as He has preserved the nation throughout history against all odds — including some modern day invasions in 1949, 1967, and 1973 — Scripture tells us that Israel will survive until the second coming of Jesus.

INCOMPREHENSIBLE CRUELTY

Although Jews have been the primary target throughout history, no people group has been immune to satanic activity. Horrible atrocities have been documented time after time, and century after century, by evil people who are responsible for the extermination of millions.

There are so many examples that I hesitate to even start. But in the twentieth century some of the most well-known are the Ukrainian genocide under Josef Stalin in the 1930's where some seven million people were killed, Adolf Hitler's Holocaust during World War II where a total of about twelve million people were exterminated (including approximately six million Jews), the "killing fields" in Cambodia under Pol Pot in the 1970's where it's estimated around two million people were murdered, and the Rwandan genocide in the 1990's where up to a million were put to death.

This has carried over into the twenty-first century with documented genocide in the Darfur region of Sudan claiming the lives of at least 400 thousand people, and the utter barbarity of Islamic radicals in the Middle East and Africa who have raped, enslaved, or murdered any non-Muslims who refuse to convert. Clearly, there is an evil behind such unconscionable brutality that is beyond what any human would even consider perpetrating in the natural.

On a more individual level, look at the horrible scourge of child and animal abuse, human trafficking, sexual assaults, murder, and other heinous examples of inhumanity. These things reinforce the understanding that there is a very evil force at work in our world. There is simply no rational explanation for why a parent would abuse their own vulnerable child, or why a stranger would use an unwilling victim for sexual gratification, or why someone would murder another who is begging for his life, or whatever true-to-life nightmare you can think of.

No person would perpetrate such vile acts of cruelty unless there was an unseen, evil influence coaxing such behavior. And that would be the powers of darkness led by none other than the spirit-realm being, Satan himself. As Paul wrote in Ephesians 2:2, these are people following the "ruler of the kingdom of the air." And John reemphasized the point when he said in 1 John 5:19 that those who are not "children of God" are "under the control of the evil one."

CONCLUDING THOUGHT

I trust by now it is clearly evident that Satan does exist, through the many biblical references to him — including the words of Paul and even Jesus Himself — to the evil activity that we see now and throughout history. For those who are still not convinced, one final question must be answered before the existence of Satan can be discounted: Where does the desire to commit hurtful actions come from?

The previously mentioned mass murderers throughout history could be accused of jealousy, insecurity, or perhaps greed. The child or animal abuser could be said to have a problem with anger. The rapist may have issues with lust or a desire for power. And the murderer could be driven by hatred. With our natural understanding, these would be logical conclusions for such illogical behaviors. But without a supernatural explanation, these conclusions still fail to meet with reason.

We are all born with a sinful nature (Psalm 51:5), but our lives are largely blank slates that are shaped for better or for worse by what we experience. Just as the direction of a teenager is heavily influenced by their peers, you could say that we as human beings are largely swayed by the company we keep in the spirit-realm. Those who choose to "make friends" with Jesus will find the fruit of the Spirit more evident in their behaviors because of His righteous influence (Galatians 5:22). Those who choose to "hang out" with Satan will find their lives more driven by the sinful nature because of his evil persuasion (Galatians 5:19-21).

So when somebody does something sacrificially good — such as a missionary who leaves a comfortable, safe life to go to an impoverished country where he or she is regularly in danger — that is evidence of a supernatural godly influence in that person's life. Conversely, when somebody does what is evil — such as those things mentioned earlier — that is evidence of a supernatural satanic influence in that person's life.

Make no mistake about it. Evil exists because Satan is real. There is really no other satisfactory explanation.

This is why eternity for the Christian is something to look forward to. After the final judgment, Satan will be thrown into hell and his ability to wreak havoc will be gone. The painful affects of sin will be no more; never again will anyone be tempted to hurt or use another. The default reaction to everything will reflect the fruit of the Spirit — love, joy, peace, patience, kindness, goodness, faithfulness, gentleness, and self-control. That's because the one who incites the sinful nature, Satan, will have been sent to "prison" for eternity by the righteous Judge, never to cause harm again.

5–GRACE GONE WILD: SOMETHING OLD

We have to understand that immeasurable love and grace make up only a part of God's nature. And the belief in Grace Gone Wild tells us that God's grace trumps every other aspect of who He is.

Like most Americans I love the old *Andy Griffith Show* reruns. In one of the episodes, high-strung Deputy Barney Fife gets a motorcycle and uses it to enforce the speed limit on a nearby highway. Before long, motorists are getting upset with Barney for his heavy-handed tactics. The truckers in particular are mad because they had always been allowed to go 5 mph above the speed limit in order to get over a steep grade. When beloved Sheriff Andy Taylor reminds his deputy of this, Barney says he wants to "nip it in the bud." He was referencing the fact that if you give them 5 mph over the speed limit now, they'll take 10, 15 or even 20 mph over the limit later.

There is actually more than one serious spiritual application that can be taken from this very funny episode. For one thing, it can actually be detrimental when rules are strictly enforced without any consideration for the circumstances. But Barney was right about one thing. If you don't "nip it in the bud" seemingly harmless behavior can eventually become dangerous.

GIVE 'EM AN INCH, THEY'LL TAKE A MILE

It's almost comical to think that Barney made such a big deal about 5 miles per hour over the speed limit. This episode was made in the early 1960's, the same time period that I was born. I grew up in a suburb of Minnesota's Twin Cities, Minneapolis and St. Paul. Before I moved to a more rural area in 1983, speed limits were mostly observed within 5 or 10 mph, even on the metro area freeways. But now when I return to visit family, I can actually see other drivers getting upset with me for staying within 5 mph of the speed limit. Ten to 15 mph over is common and enforcement up to that point is rare. Barney would be appalled!

At the same time, law enforcement officials will tell you that speeding is a major factor in traffic accidents involving serious injuries and deaths. There is no telling how much heartache could have been avoided if Barney's admonition to "nip it in the bud" would have been followed to this day. Instead, a *little* grace shown by some officers has become a *lot* of grace and the result has been tragic for countless individuals and their families.

Perhaps you've already gotten the point of this analogy. God's grace is a valuable and necessary component of our lives as Christians because we are imperfect people. We *need* grace. But when our understanding of God's grace is taken too far, it can be detrimental to the point of physical and spiritual danger. And that is what I call "Grace Gone Wild."

ANCIENT ROOTS OF A MODERN TEACHING

I was talking with a Christian brother not too long ago about a man I'll call Vern. I explained that when Vern was young, he accepted Jesus as his Savior in the usual way. He felt the tug of the Holy Spirit on his heart, repented of his sins, and confessed with his mouth that he was a Christian. But later, Vern's sister went through a painful cancer death. He blamed God for what his sister had to suffer and he became an enemy to Christianity from that time on. I explained that Vern has spent his remaining years doing whatever he can to discredit the message of Christ and to convince as many people as possible to reject Him.

I told my friend that according to the message of Grace Gone Wild Vern would still be going to heaven. To my surprise, he said that under the circumstances he would agree that Vern *will* be going to heaven because he had made a previous proclamation of faith in Jesus. I was rather shocked at my friend's response. Because in my mind, for this to be true, one would have to believe that Vern will be dragged kicking and screaming into heaven to spend eternity with a God he hates and has battled against for decades.

A belief such as this is fueled at least in part by a very common teaching within the Kingdom today, one which I would say over-extends the reach of God's grace. This is an extremely popular teaching so I want to do a little disclaimer before I discuss it. I tend to cringe at this belief because I have seen it used by some people to justify lifestyles that are very sinful and destructive. But because it is so common among Christians today I want to preface my remarks by saying please keep reading, even if just out of morbid curiosity.

No matter how well-accepted it is, I would submit that Scripture does not back this teaching. I know many of you will disagree with me, at least at the start. It is taught in some very good churches by some very solid brothers and sisters in Christ so it may seem almost sacrilegious to consider a different viewpoint. All I ask is that you read through my dissenting arguments with an open mind. Then do what I have to do regularly — ask the Holy Spirit to speak into your heart and mind what God's truth really is on the subject. After all, that should be our goal on this or any other disputed issue. (I don't know about you, but I don't want to win an argument if in the end I am actually wrong!)

The teaching I am speaking of is the belief in "eternal security," often referred to as "once saved, always saved." Some denominations teach that once you proclaim Jesus as your Savior, as in the example of Vern above, then you are saved from that moment on no matter how you choose to live your life. This is a belief popularized some five hundred years ago by John Calvin, which coincides with his teaching on election and predestination that we discussed in chapter three.

Other denominations have a different take on eternal security, teaching that once you are baptized as a baby or adult you are heaven-bound from that time on. This belief actually predated Calvin by about twelve centuries. In the late 300's AD, the influential bishop Augustine — who is responsible for much of what is accepted as Catholic doctrine today — introduced this teaching into the church of his day. It survived the Reformation and became an oft-believed part of Protestant doctrine as well.

THE INSECURITY OF ETERNAL SECURITY

Although the belief in eternal security has been around for many centuries, it has really only become the predominant belief among Christians within the last eighty years or so. And it has seemed to gain momentum in this age of Grace Gone Wild. This would make sense. Because when we place so much emphasis on the love and grace aspect of God's nature, then naturally we would believe there is absolutely nothing we could do to put our eternal fellowship with Him at risk.

When I am teaching or preaching I try to pay attention not so much to what I am saying, but rather, what the listener might be hearing. There is a well-known preacher who beats the eternal security drum pretty hard, and I have heard him say on occasion, "You can't out-sin the love of God." While this is true, in context with what he is preaching I can imagine many people are hearing in their minds, "so go ahead, give it a try!" It's almost as if permission has just been granted to ignore biblical commands and live free of any godly restraint.

Now clearly this is not going to be the reaction of everyone, and probably not most of those hearing that message. But there are unquestionably those who *are* going to respond in just that way. Perhaps you can already see how spiritually dangerous the belief in eternal security can be, not just for the person himself because of his questionable salvation status, but because of the potential damage he can do to other lives as well.

I was talking with a church-going man one time who was having an affair with a married woman. I asked him, "Aren't you concerned about risking your salvation because of your unrepentant sin?" He promptly and proudly responded, "Oh, I know where I'm going when I die." His obvious implication was that "you can't out-sin the love of God" so he had no worries about his eternal destiny.

When the truth came out about the affair, this man ended up causing untold pain to everybody involved including the woman, her children, and the victimized husband. According to eternal security theology, this man will not be held ultimately accountable for this affair or — as I found out later — for at least one other immoral relationship he was a part of. He was literally using his "once saved, always saved" belief as permission in his mind to use people and gratify his sinful desires.

Now I realize this man likely experienced some consequences for his actions here on this earth. And I also know it's possible that he could eventually sincerely repent and be forgiven of his sins. But the fact of the matter is, the damage had already been done. Because of his belief in eternal security, this man left behind a trail of destruction made up of broken hearts and devastated lives. As a self-professed Christian, he also brought damage to the reputation of Christ — and God only knows how many lives may have been eternally impacted for the worst because of his actions.

THE GRACE OF JUSTICE

We have to understand that immeasurable love and grace make up only a part of God's nature. The belief in Grace Gone Wild tells us that God's grace trumps every other aspect of who He is. For instance, God is also a God of justice. Let's say I was the victimized husband in the previous example. If I didn't know that justice was a steadfast attribute of God, there would be no way I could forgive this man or my wife. Would there be any way

I could ever hope to forgive if I believed God would treat such a felonious offense as a misdemeanor?

Could you see an earthly judge at the trial say, "Well, my son already took the penalty for this offense, so I will let the perpetrators go free without punishment." What? Would that be justice? Of course not! In the same way, our Heavenly Judge would not ignore their violation. After all, He hates the sins committed against us even more than we do.

Yes, God is a God of perfect love and perfect grace, but He's also a God of perfect justice. Would the punishment be an eternity in hell? It would all depend on those who committed the sin. It would be up to them whether or not they would choose to sincerely repent and turn from their wicked ways. If they did, then the Bible says the blood of Jesus would cover that sin and God would see it no more. But one way or another, God would assure that perfect justice was done, whether here on earth or in eternity.

MISPLACED SALVATION?

Of course, my belief that the doctrine of eternal security is dangerous doesn't matter if it is in fact truth. So again we have to head to the Scriptures, because anything we believe about anything is only opinion unless it matches the truth found in God's Word.

I often hear eternal security proponents say, "You can't lose your salvation." And you know what? I agree with them. John 10:27-29 says:

My sheep listen to my voice; I know them, and they follow me. I give them eternal life, and they shall never perish; no one can snatch them out of my hand. My Father, who has given them to me, is greater than all; no one can snatch them out of my Father's hand.

So based on verses such as these, I believe you can't *lose* your salvation. When you lose something it is not by choice and it can be very troubling depending on the value of what you have lost.

But I do believe you can choose to *reject* your salvation and, at least initially, be at peace with the decision.

When you accept Jesus as your Savior and Lord in the first place, it is no accident. It is a choice you are making. And just as you once chose to accept Jesus, you can choose to reject Him. The free will that God has given to us does not get nullified just because we become Christians. As the wonderful hymn "Come Thou Fount of Every Blessing" says: "Prone to wander Lord I feel it, prone to leave the God I love." When we are saved Satan does not give up his attempts to turn our devotion away from God and we need to guard against his attacks.

The book of Hebrews has many warnings against personal apostasy, or falling away from faith in God. And there are some very sober warnings for doing so. Hebrews 6:4-6 says:

> It is impossible for those who have once been enlightened, who have tasted the heavenly gift, who have shared in the Holy Spirit, who have tasted the goodness of the word of God and the powers of the coming age, if they fall away, to be brought back to repentance, because to their loss they are crucifying the Son of God all over again and subjecting him to public disgrace.

The author of Hebrews is leaving no doubt here that he is talking about someone who was at one time a committed follower of Jesus but has "fallen away." In verse 8 he compares such a person to a worthless land in danger of being cursed – a land that in the end will be burned. And later in Hebrews 10:26-29:

> If we deliberately keep on sinning after we have received the knowledge of the truth, no sacrifice for sins is left, but only a fearful expectation of judgment and of raging fire that will consume the enemies of God. Anyone who rejected the law of Moses died without mercy on the testimony of two or three witnesses. How much more severely do you think a man deserves to be punished who has trampled the Son of God under foot, who has treated as

an unholy thing the blood of the covenant that sanctified him, and who has insulted the Spirit of grace?

Again there is no doubt that the author is talking about someone who had previously proclaimed faith in Jesus, who had "received the knowledge of the truth," and then turned away. These verses do not appear in any way to leave room for a belief in eternal security. In fact, the author of Hebrews encourages the reader in 10:36, 39 not to put their future salvation in jeopardy:

You need to persevere so that when you have done the will of God, you will receive what he has promised...But we are not of those who shrink back and are destroyed, but of those who believe and are saved.

FREE WILL REMAINS

Eternal security advocates put a significant emphasis on the verses relating to Christians being marked with a seal when we accept Jesus as our Savior. For example, in 2 Corinthians 1:21-22, Paul wrote:

Now it is God who makes both us and you stand firm in Christ. He anointed us, set his seal of ownership on us, and put his Spirit in our hearts as a deposit, guaranteeing what is to come.

And again in Ephesians 1:13-14:

Having believed, you were marked in him with a seal, the promised Holy Spirit, who is a deposit guaranteeing our inheritance until the redemption of those who are God's possession–to the praise of his glory.

These verses talk about God putting a seal of ownership on us, which is the Holy Spirit. When we accept Jesus as our Savior, the Holy Spirit comes to dwell in us at that moment. As I've mentioned previously, the Holy Spirit does not force Himself on anyone. He only comes to dwell in the person who invites Him in. And this is glorious news for those of us who are truly desiring to live, learn, and grow in our relationship with the Lord. We know that we are His, and nothing can steal us away from Him. We are safe in His arms for eternity.

However, as I have also previously said, the Holy Spirit is a gentleman. Just as He will only dwell within the person who invites Him in, so too He will only stay where He is welcome. Remember the earlier example of Vern? He had accepted Jesus as his Savior at one point in his life, but after a painful experience, spent the rest of his life fighting against Christianity at every opportunity. In such a case, the Holy Spirit is not going to stay in a dwelling where the owner is trying to kick Him out. The Holy Spirit loves Vern so He will be grieving as He leaves. But free will is not voided just because at one time a person professes faith in Christ. And unless the Holy Spirit is invited to return before Vern dies, his eternal destiny will be hell.

Vern's story reminds me of the Parable of the Sower in Matthew 13. Jesus talked of a farmer who sowed seed. Some of the seed fell on rocky places where there wasn't much soil. The plants sprang up quickly because the soil was shallow, but they also scorched quickly in the sun because they had no root. When Jesus explains the meaning of the parable, we can see in verses 20 and 21 that this is analogous of men like Vern...

> The one who received the seed that fell on the rocky places is the man who hears the word and at once receives it with joy. But since he has no root, he lasts only a short time. When trouble or persecution comes because of the word, he quickly falls away.

I once had a friend say to me that he has a kind of hybrid belief about eternal security. He said true believers in Christ would never turn away; that a guy like Vern may have *thought* he was a Christian, but as it turns out, didn't ever really believe. This may be true for some people, but the Parable of the Sower shows this is certainly not always the case. The man in the above verses heard the word "and at once received it with joy." That sounds like a true believer to me. But for many who don't get a firm foundation established early in their faith, they "quickly fall away" when trials come.

This is why it is critical to teach the full counsel of God right from the start, including the understanding that being a Christian means not only great blessings now and for eternity thanks to the grace of God, but also trials and tribulations because of His desire to see us grow and mature in our faith. Besides, Satan is very upset about losing a soul and he wants it back. So he's going to attack the baby Christian at every opportunity, hoping they might turn away from their new-found faith. If God's grace is overemphasized to the new believer, they may question the validity of Christianity when harsh or painful difficulties make it appear His grace is absent.

EDITING THE BOOK OF LIFE

When a person becomes a new believer in Jesus, the Bible tells us that God writes their name in what is called the "book of life." It is a glorious moment, and all heaven rejoices (Luke 15:7). But it is also very sad to think that many will reject God's gift of salvation to the very end. In Revelation 20:15 we are told that at the final judgment: "If anyone's name was not found written in the book of life, he was thrown into the lake of fire."

The "lake of fire" is of course a description of the eternal hell. And only those whose names were written in God's book of life were saved. The doctrine of eternal security would say that once a name is written in that book it can never be removed. But very early and very late in the Bible, we are told that the names of God's children which were once written in His book of life can be "blotted out." In Exodus 32:31-33 it says:

> So Moses went back to the Lord and said, "Oh, what a great sin these people have committed! They have made themselves gods of gold. But now, please forgive their sin–but if not, then blot me out of the book you have written." The Lord replied to Moses, "Whoever has sinned against me I will blot out of my book."

The Hebrews had committed a grievous sin and Moses was pleading with the Lord to hold him accountable in their place. But God made sure Moses knew that only the disobedient would be at risk of being removed from His book of life because of their choice to live in unrepentant sin.

We also see near the end of the Bible, in the book of Revelation, that those who walk away from their faithfulness to God can have their names removed from His book of life. John is writing what he is being shown while "in the Spirit." In the first three chapters of Revelation, he relays messages that Jesus has for seven churches located in Asia.

The individual churches were experiencing the issues being written about at that time. But there are different beliefs today about what these churches actually represent theologically. Some believe the churches were placed in a particular order in Revelation so as to chronologically represent different eras in Christian history. Others believe they are representative of the types of churches that are always present at any given time. I have a somewhat hybrid belief on this.

I believe the characteristics of the churches have been individually more prevalent at certain times in history, but also that each of the church types has been alive and well at any given time. For instance, the church in Pergamum had many similarities to the twenty-first century churches we are seeing in America today.

The church in Pergamum (Revelation 2:12-17) was located in an evil society "where Satan has his throne." In the midst of persecution, many in the church remained faithful to their witness for Christ. But there was also false teaching that condoned idolatry and sexual immorality. In our American churches today there are many who are remaining faithful to biblical truth regardless of the attacks against them. But there are also a significant number who are being deceived into believing that idolatrous and sexually immoral behavior is actually acceptable despite the clear directives in the Bible. (These Kingdom invaders will be discussed in chapters to come.)

The church in Sardis was a spiritually dead church and Jesus exhorted them — through John's writing — to wake up, obey, and repent. He said there were a few in the church who had remained faithful, and they were described as wearing clothes that were white and unsoiled. But in Revelation 3:4-5 Jesus made it clear that those who had turned away from the faith will not join in their reward:

> Yet you have a few people in Sardis who have not soiled their clothes. They walk with me, dressed in white, for they are worthy. He who overcomes will, like them, be dressed in white. I will never blot out his name from the book of life, but will acknowledge his name before my Father and his angels.

From these verses, we see that God would not consider even for a moment blotting the faithful out of His book of life. Conversely, it stands to reason that the opposite is true; those who have chosen to walk away from their faith can have their name removed unless they repent and "overcome" before their death. Please think about this for a moment. Would there be any reason for this passage to even mention anyone being blotted out or removed from the book of life unless it is indeed a possibility?

A MILLENNIAL DILEMMA FOR ETERNAL SECURITY

While we're still in the book of Revelation, I'd like to point out one final thought on the issue of eternal security that doesn't seem to stand up to biblical scrutiny. Chapter 20 talks about the Millennium, or thousand-year reign of Christ after the Great Tribulation. Satan is bound in an abyss during this period "to keep him from deceiving the nations." Then at the end of the Millennium, he is released one last time to lead a rebellion.

There is some dispute among theologians as to exactly what will happen during the Millennium. But the general consensus is that the resurrected and raptured Christians will return to earth to rule and reign with Jesus during this period. They will have glorified, spiritual bodies. The people subject to rule will be those who accepted Christ during the Tribulation and survived to the end. These people will still have their mortal bodies and will get married and have children just as we do today. Because the effects of sin will be removed with Satan's incarceration, people will live for hundreds of years — if not the full thousand years — and the population will grow dramatically. It may reach or surpass even what we have on the earth today.

There are different interpretations of what I'm about to say, but I believe without the temptations of Satan and his demons, any sins committed during the Millennium would likely be sins of omission rather than sins of rebellion. In other words, they would be the type of sins a person may commit because of a lack of knowledge rather than with purposeful rebellion against God. After all, why do we sin? It is either because we are ignorant of God's commands or because we rebel against the commands that we know. People also give in to sin because of overwhelming addictions. But without the spirit-realm temptation that causes uncontrolled behavior, addictive sins will also be absent during this time.

So this prompts a dilemma for the doctrine of eternal security. The children born during the Millennium will be taught the truth about Jesus from their earliest days and witness His goodness in every aspect of their lives. There will be no rebellion in them without the spiritual powers of darkness to tempt them. I believe this is why Satan is released at the end of the thousand years and allowed to cast his deception upon mankind one last time. As I've mentioned previously, God is a God of perfect justice and even children born during the Millennium must make the same choice as all of mankind — to either become and remain a child of God or reject him.

There really is no other logical explanation for why God would release Satan briefly before the final judgment. Now if these children born during the Millennium — of whom most have grown well into adulthood — can be deceived into turning against God at this point, then it stands to reason that anyone can choose to reject their salvation just as they chose to accept it in the first place. And there are many who will turn from God at that time. Revelation 20:8-10 says:

> In number they are like the sand on the seashore. They marched across the breadth of the earth and surrounded the camp of God's people, the city he loves. But fire came down from heaven and devoured them. And the devil, who deceived them, was thrown into the lake of burning sulfur...

These people could have remained in the security of this utopian Kingdom. But they chose to believe Satan's lies and threw it all away to their eternal detriment. This is really no different from when a Christian today lives in the knowledge of God's glorious truth and eventually chooses to reject it based on satanic lies.

CONCLUDING THOUGHT

As I said at the beginning of the discussion about eternal security, I believe this teaching has contributed to the problem of Grace Gone Wild. I have seen this belief used by some people to justify very sinful and destructive lifestyles that have caused great pain and potentially eternal consequences. All I ask is that you consider my arguments with an open mind and pray about what God's truth really is on the subject.

No matter what point in history a person lives, it is obvious that Satan's ability to deceive never wavers and we can never let down our guard. We have to be aware of his plots, including false teachings, that can lead to rebellion against God and His commands — even after we accept Jesus as our Savior. Whether you believe in eternal security or not, I encourage you to be wary of any grace-heavy teaching that gives you permission to go against God's clearly expressed instructions in Scripture. Instead, I urge you to embrace those things which inspire you toward a greater holiness and consecration to God.

6–GRACE GONE WILD:
SOMETHING NEW

*Jesus is calling those who would follow Him to surrender
their lives completely. This is a concept that has been
largely forgotten in today's Christian culture. Sadly, the
message of grace is now proclaimed so loudly that it has
often silenced the ever-important call for devotion.*

I have a confession to make — I have a major sweet tooth. My
favorite breakfasts are toaster pastries, frosted of course, and
sugar-sweetened cereals. In fact, I even add sugar to some sugar-sweetened cereals! And my coffee? Let's just say if it still
tastes like coffee I haven't yet added enough flavored creamer
and sugar. During the so-called Great Recession that began in
2008, the general manager at our radio network asked the staff
to start paying for some items that had been provided free up to
that point to help get us through the economic downturn. And
I'm convinced we were able to survive without laying anybody
off because I started paying for my own sugar.

Now I'm obviously exaggerating, but it is true that I have
always enjoyed sweets more than is good for me. There came
a time however when I realized, for the sake of my health, that
I needed to cut back on my sugar consumption. As good as the
sweet stuff tasted, I knew I needed to add more in the way of
fruits, vegetables, and lean meats in order to have a healthy, well-
rounded diet.

In the same way, I believe a lot of what we hear from our Christian leaders these days is too heavy on spiritual "sweets." We are hearing the good stuff about grace, mercy, love, and forgiveness — which is absolutely critical to a proper understanding of God and the Christian life — but we are not being told enough about the other essentials needed to have a healthy, well-rounded theological diet. Among them is striving to live a life of obedience to God according to the Scriptures.

THERE'S SOMETHING TO BE SAID FOR FEAR

The biggest problem with any sugary-sweet teaching that overemphasizes God's grace is that it removes any fear of Him. While some would say that is a good thing, the Bible would disagree. In both Psalm 111:10 and Proverbs 9:10 we find these words: "The fear of the Lord is the beginning of wisdom."

The fear of the Lord is a topic you don't hear a lot about these days from church leaders. It's just not a popular thing to talk about in our grace-saturated Christian culture. But the verses above are among many in the Bible pointing to the wisdom in having a healthy fear of the Lord. I call it "healthy" because it is not a cowering type of fear where I'm afraid I'll get squashed by God if I displease Him. That would be "Fear Gone Wild" which is also a dangerous extreme.

In fact, I tend to believe that an unhealthy emphasis on "hellfire and brimstone" preaching in the early part of the twentieth century was a contributing factor to today's excessive focus on grace. It led many people to a concern that if they went "one sin too far" they might end up in hell. You can imagine how terrifying this could have been, particularly for young children. This non-biblical belief was then replaced in ensuing generations by the aforementioned "you can't out-sin the love of God." It has been my observation that human beings are prone to knee-jerk reactions as a way of responding to perceived injustices. This appears to be exactly what has happened here.

Psalm 103:8-10 says a great deal about the grace that God extends to us:

> The Lord is compassionate and gracious, slow to anger, abounding in love. He will not always accuse, nor will he harbor his anger forever; he does not treat us as our sins deserve or repay us according to our iniquities.

The line "he does not treat us as our sins deserve" could be a definition of mercy. And grace goes a step further — we get good things we do not deserve, including eternal life through Jesus Christ. His sacrifice on a cross means that God does not "repay us according to our iniquities." But in order to have balance, we need to take this in context with the verses that follow, Psalm 103:11-13 and 17-18:

> For as high as the heavens are above the earth, so great is his love for those who fear him; as far as the east is from the west, so far has he removed our transgressions from us. As a father has compassion on his children, so the Lord has compassion on those who fear him...But from everlasting to everlasting the Lord's love is with those who fear him, and his righteousness with their children's children — with those who keep his covenant and remember to obey his precepts.

Here, David draws a correlation no less than three times between God's love for His children and their appropriate fear of Him, followed by their subsequent obedience.

WAIT 'TIL YOUR FATHER GETS HOME!

I have a wonderful, loving earthly father which has helped me relate better to what this passage of Scripture is talking about. Sadly, I know that's not the case with way too many people. For them, understanding God and His nature is not easy because their earthly father has been abusive, neglectful, or absent from their lives. But my dad has been a great help in understanding God's love for me. He has been there for me when I have faced trouble, rejoiced with me in successes, and stood by me through life's deepest trials.

My father has also disciplined me when I have needed it. During my formative years, when I was doing something I knew was wrong, I feared that my dad would punish me if he found out. It was a healthy fear that developed over time as I knew justified consequences followed improper behavior. This helped me understand how God's discipline works.

My respect for my earthly father grew stronger because I knew he loved me enough to not only bless me when my behavior was appropriate, but to discipline me when I disobeyed. And the same thing has happened over the years in my relationship with my heavenly Father. I believe a healthy fear of the Lord could be characterized as a respect with such depth that it would be unreasonable if it were reserved for anyone other than God Himself.

WHO ARE YOU GOING TO LIVE FOR?

Now I absolutely agree that God loves us no matter what we do. But a comprehensive understanding of Christianity means there is significant responsibility that comes with the choice to make Jesus our Savior. Because the Bible tells us that He is also to become our *Lord*. When someone is your lord, it means your life belongs to them and living for them is more important than living for yourself. In Mark 8:34-35 Jesus says:

> If anyone would come after me, he must deny himself and take up his cross and follow me. For whoever wants to save his life will lose it, but whoever loses his life for me and for the gospel will save it.

Jesus is calling those who would follow Him to surrender their lives completely. This is a concept that has been largely forgotten in today's Christian culture.

When I was young, I remember going to church not only for the main Sunday morning service but also for Sunday school, vibrant Sunday night services, and Wednesday night Bible studies.

Today, many churches have dropped all but their main Sunday service, usually because of a lack of attendance. I find this to be a very discouraging trend. I recall learning many important spiritual lessons in the more personal Sunday school and Bible study settings. And the Sunday night services were something special. I can remember the Holy Spirit manifesting Himself in very special ways as people would head to the altars seeking more of the Lord. Many felt a call to the ministry, including myself.

But sadly, the message of grace is now proclaimed so loudly that it has often silenced the ever-important call for devotion. I recall a couple of conversations I had in recent years with two fathers who were well-meaning but, I feel, misguided by the grace-heavy teaching of our day.

One was divorced and only had custody of his son on certain weekends. So rather than go to church on some Sunday mornings, this dad would take his son fishing so they could spend some quality time together. On the surface, this sounded like a wonderful idea birthed by a loving father. But if you dig a little deeper, what was the message being sent to his son? If anything else he was being unintentionally taught that church attendance is optional and has limited importance.

The other father stopped attending Sunday night services as his sons got older because he called that their "family night." They would stay home and watch movies or play games. Again, on the surface, it seemed like a good idea. But a similar message was being sent to his sons about the limited value of going to church. A family night of secular pursuits was deemed more important than a night of growing together spiritually.

This is not uncommon today. According to a Barna Group study conducted in early 2011, a staggering 59 percent of 18-29 year olds who grew up in Christian homes no longer attend church. Could this be explained, at least in part, by an unintentional message being sent to children that a sincere devotion to their faith is optional? I just can't help but wonder how much better things might be in our culture today if we had continued emphasizing the importance of gathering together as believers, spending time with God at every opportunity, and inviting Him to mold us into effective vessels of service for the Kingdom.

DESTITUTE PROSPERITY

Unfortunately that type of commitment to Christ is becoming increasingly rare, and it is being overtaken by a more self-serving kind of faith. There has been a teaching around for several decades called the Prosperity Doctrine in which believers are told that, as children of the King, they deserve the riches of the Kingdom. So hoarding wealth and living a life of luxury gets the stamp of approval. I believe a correlation can be drawn between this doctrine and the more recent emphasis on Grace Gone Wild.

In the beginning, God created man in His image. But both the Prosperity Doctrine and Grace Gone Wild tend to create God in *our* image. In other words, we believe that God loves us so immensely that He would want us to always be wealthy and happy. And He would never require us to leave our comfort zone.

Rather than lead us to a life of progressive sanctification, in the end these teachings basically turn Christianity into a more desirable set of beliefs — giving permission to read and know God's commandments and then ignore them, if we choose, to live the more abundant life as *we* see it. It's like getting dessert without ever having to eat your fruits and vegetables.

But sadly, this does not reflect truth. The Old Testament book of Ecclesiastes was written by Solomon, a man who learned this lesson well. He was healthy, wealthy, and wise. And he took advantage of every good thing life had to offer — from those that were pleasing to God, to those that were downright sinful. After all of his experiences, Solomon wrote his final thoughts in Ecclesiastes 12:13: "Now all has been heard; here is the conclusion of the matter. Fear God and keep his commandments, for this is the whole duty of man."

This pretty well sums up what the Christian life should be all about. But beyond Scripture, there is one very obvious reason that the Prosperity Doctrine and the message of Grace Gone Wild lack credibility. Both beliefs really only work in affluent, free societies like the United States. Despite recent declines, the U.S. still has had one of the wealthiest economies in the history of the world over the last several decades along with significant religious freedoms. These two factors have combined to make for a life of relative ease and safety for American Christians. The result has been a more self-focused religiosity that has not required a wholehearted devotion to Christ.

PROSPEROUS DESTITUTION

It is easy to talk about God's desire for you to be wealthy when there is affluence all around you. Try selling the Prosperity Doctrine to Christians in an impoverished country. I had the opportunity to go on a couple of short-term missions trips in 1979 and 1981 — one to Spain and the other to Mexico. In both countries, I saw poverty that I had never witnessed before in my life. And I had the privilege of meeting many brothers and sisters in Christ who had virtually nothing.

One couple I remember in particular lived in a shanty in the Mexico City area. They had several children as I recall, and their dwelling was probably no bigger than the living room of my parents' house where I was residing at the time. The Prosperity Doctrine would imply that these people were somehow missing out on the wealth that God wants to give them, maybe because of ignorance or perhaps some unconfessed sin in their lives.

But the strange thing was, they were extraordinarily joyful and content like I had rarely seen in American Christians. After several years it began to occur to me that they, and people like them all over the world, are the ones who are truly wealthy. When the Bible discusses prosperity it is not a monetary wealth per se. It can be, but more often than not it is a life that is abundant in peace, joy and contentedness. How would you rather live?

Loaded with money but full of anxiety and strife? Or poor as the world sees it but experiencing the "peace that passes under-standing" through an intimacy with God.

We have all heard of famous athletes and movie stars who have committed suicide. They basically had everything the world had to offer, yet still felt life wasn't worth living. If only they had read the book of Ecclesiastes and discovered along with Solomon that the meaninglessness of life is removed when you choose to live for the Lord.

These Mexican believers knew this. They had almost nothing as far as material wealth, and yet they had come to the realization that when Jesus is all you have, He is all you need. And despite their lack of wealth, they were at peace knowing that God would supply all of their needs according to His glorious riches in Christ Jesus (Philippians 4:19). Sadly, in our comparatively affluent society we have largely missed this point.

SHACKLED YET FREE

In terms of religious freedom, do you think our brothers and sisters in Christ who are facing severe persecution because of their faith are focused on a self-serving grace? In many countries being a Christian means real sacrifice. In Muslim-majority coun-tries in particular it can mean heavy taxation, imprisonment, or even death for not renouncing Jesus as your Savior. This tends to separate the real believers from those who accept Christ as "fire insurance" to simply avoid hell, or who practice a cultural Christianity which makes church merely a place of feel-good fellowship.

When our faith truly costs us something, that is when our relationship with God grows in intimacy and we become more effective vessels of service for Him. Many years ago a missionary to a communist country during the cold war came to our church and shared with us that the persecuted believers in that country weren't asking him to encourage Americans to pray for them.

He said they were actually praying for us — that God would not allow Satan to use our lack of suffering to make us complacent.

Can you wrap your mind around that? They literally looked at their harsh reality as a blessing because it made them powerful and effective servants. As they were faithful in the midst of their suffering, God proved Himself to be consistently faithful to them and it made them steadfast and strong no matter what they faced. Again, this reality is largely missed in a society with significant religious freedoms. Interestingly enough, in China — where any religious freedom is a government smokescreen and the real Church is underground — Christianity has grown exponentially in recent decades. At the same time, it has stagnated and even begun a decline in North America and Europe where calling yourself by Christ's name has been relatively persecution free.

When we are able to focus so much on God's grace without seeing the whole picture of what it means to take up our cross and follow Jesus, it tends to create a weak and ineffective church. Sadly, I believe this is becoming more and more evident in our society today. We have an abundant number of churches here in the U.S., Christian radio and television 24-7, and a plethora of Christian books, magazines, websites, etc. Yet statistics show that each generation is becoming more accepting of behaviors that go against biblical instruction, and less interested in church and Christianity — let alone living out their faith in a godly way.

THE IDOL OF GRACE

It seems that the grace of God has almost become an idol for many Christians. I was talking with a pastor one time after a service in which he said some things that disturbed me. He spoke of the grace of God and the resulting freedom in Christ in terms that I believed really gave people license to sin. I know that wasn't his intention. Nevertheless — as I mentioned earlier — it's not so much what we say that is important, but rather, what people hear. I shared my concerns with him, including my beliefs related to the excesses of Grace Gone Wild, and he seemed to light up. He blurted out with a positive twist, "I believe in Grace Gone Wild too!" He then added with a kumbaya-like awe, "God's grace is so immense we can't even comprehend it."

Within a month I was talking with another man about the topic — I'll call him William — and he expressed the same sentiment with almost the exact starry-eyed passion, "God's grace is beyond what we can possibly comprehend!" Within the next few months, I heard similar words from other people as well.

I thought about this for a while and it began to occur to me that grace has become almost a capital "G" word for these people and others like them. It appears that the grace of God may be as much an object of their worship as God Himself. Because of this, it seems their focus is on emphasizing what we *can* do as Christians as opposed to what we *should* do as Christians. This type of mindset would naturally tend to prevent spiritual growth.

GRACE AND THE REALITY OF HUMAN NATURE

Those who are excessively focused on grace will often say this attribute of God will inevitably cause us to live obediently because we desire to show our gratitude to Him. This is undoubtedly true for many Christians. But for a significant number of people this belief actually defies human nature.

As in the example of Barney Fife and the motorcycle in the last chapter, we have seen motorists increase their average speeds over the last few decades because of the extra grace shown by law enforcement officers. Would we really see people driving an average of 5, 10, and even 15 mph over the speed limit today if they knew they would get a ticket for doing so? The average person, if they were being honest, would say they are more motivated to go the speed limit because they don't want to get a ticket rather than because it is the right thing to do. That would include Christians.

How many of us when we were growing up were actually motivated to obey our parents simply because we wanted to please them? Or was there an understanding, whether consciously or not, that discipline would follow disobedient behavior? In school, were you motivated to get assignments done because your teacher was so kind, or was it more because you didn't want to face the negative consequences if your class work wasn't completed? And personally, I can testify to the fact that fear of being sent to the principal's office kept me from doing a lot of stupid things I might have otherwise done.

So like it or not, it's important to understand that even as Christians we are motivated in part by the knowledge that inappropriate behavior leads to discipline. Paul wrote in Romans 2:4-6:

> God's kindness leads you toward repentance. But because of your stubbornness and your unrepentant heart, you are storing up wrath against yourself for the day of God's wrath, when his righteous judgment will be revealed. God will give to each person according to what he has done.

It would be nice if our relationships with God could be all about rewards. But that's simply not reality. Just as earthly parents have to discipline a disobedient child to assure he grows into a respectful, responsible adult, so too our heavenly Father has to discipline His children when necessary to help us grow into the mature Christians we ought to be.

TAKING THE GOD OF GRACE FOR GRANTED

Ironically, when God's attribute of grace is overemphasized it actually leads to God Himself being taken for granted. As an example, look at what happens in a typical home. Even in a loving family, we often say and do things in a conflict that we would not when we are with others. For instance, I rarely have a heated discussion with co-workers, those at church, or in the marketplace. I attempt to use all of my problem-solving skills to bring positive resolution to any conflict. But at home, it is so much easier to impulsively respond to emotions with my wife or kids rather than use the measured response that would be likely elsewhere. And I know I'm not alone.

Why is that? In large part it's because it is easy to take our relationships at home for granted. We know our loved ones will show us more grace than others would, and that our family relationships have an additional level of security no matter what ill-advised things we might say or do. So whether it's our intention or not, we end up treating them differently. I know this isn't the situation in all homes — some individuals respond much better and others much worse — but this is clearly a typical situation.

This applies to all ages. Many years ago my wife and I were asked by a couple at our church to babysit their three boys, all of whom were under ten years of age. During the evening that we were watching them, they were well-behaved and remarkably enjoyable to have around. But the minute their parents returned the boys went through a transformation, becoming rather demanding and disrespectful. The mother seemed apologetic about leaving the boys with us, but we told her in all honesty it was a pleasure to take care of them.

I have seen this type of double-standard played out time and time again in family dynamics. These boys didn't know where they stood with me and my wife. How much misbehavior would we tolerate? And what would be the consequence if they did go too far? So their unconscious response was to behave very appropriately just to be on the safe side. But when their parents returned, again without consciously thinking about it, their natural response was to press the limits because they knew exactly how far they could go before facing discipline. Without knowing it, they were demanding an excessive measure of grace from their parents.

There often is a similar dynamic in our relationships with God. He is our heavenly Father so there is a supernatural family connection and we often take Him for granted knowing the depths of His amazing grace.

Now in reality, is it acceptable to treat our family members with less care and respect just because they will show us more grace? Of course not. As I've grown older I have matured as a man, but more importantly as a Christian, to the point where it's far less often I could be accused of taking the grace of my family for granted. The same should be said for the relationships that each one of us has with God. As the days, months, and years go by, we should continue to see progress in the care and respect we show to God and His commands — a spiritual maturity that no longer requires an excessive measure of His grace.

THE LIMITS OF GOD'S GRACE

Sometimes in a family, tough love is needed when destructive behaviors do not change. There has to be a limit to the grace shown to a family member who is endangering himself or his family. Ongoing drug and alcohol abuse, a gambling addiction, an unfaithful spouse, verbal or physical abuse; these are just some of the behaviors that would require tough love to send a non-negotiable message that change is required. Depending on the level of severity and danger to the family, tough love could consist of leaving the offender at least for a time, mental health or law enforcement intervention, or a forced removal from the home at the direction of the courts.

Similarly, there is a limit to God's grace. I made that comment to William, one of the men I mentioned earlier, and he had a very hard time accepting that. I have a great deal of respect for William even though we don't always see eye to eye, and this is the type of statement I don't want to make haphazardly unless I'm sure. So I made a point of carefully considering and praying about it, and I continue to feel it is valid.

In my own life, I would say I had taken advantage of God's grace for about thirty years. I was a Christian, but there was a lot in my life that did not represent Christ well. And then God allowed me to go through some very emotionally painful experiences. Looking back, I feel like He was saying, "You have taken advantage of My grace long enough. You call yourself by My name, now it's time to live like My child."

God used tough love on me and I'm very grateful. That was the point at which I recommitted my life to Him. I became a better husband, father, and Christian; basically a better man overall. If I had chosen to rebel against His discipline, I dare say my future — and even my eternity — would likely have been disastrously bleak. And my family would have been among the victims of my selfishness. But because of my choice to submit to Him, God extended His precious grace to me, and indirectly, to those I love so dearly.

Glaring Old Testament examples of the limits of God's grace can be seen in the ultimate destruction of whole people groups. At the instruction of the Lord, Moses wrote to the Israelites in Deuteronomy 20:16-18:

> However, in the cities of the nations the Lord your God is giving you as an inheritance, do not leave anything that breathes. Completely destroy them–the Hittites, Amorites, Canaanites, Perizzites, Hivites, and Jebusites– as the Lord your God has commanded you. Otherwise, they will teach you to follow all the detestable things they do in worshiping their gods, and you will sin against the Lord your God.

These verses have been difficult for many people to accept throughout the centuries. How could a loving God of grace decree the annihilation of thousands of people? Even though it is prior to the New Covenant under Jesus, this still seems brutal to the extreme — far from the nature of the God we know and love as Christians. But with the benefit of historical reflection, we can see that God in His omniscience understood that these people groups had become morally corrupt to the point of no return. Archeological evidence supports what verse 18 says; these people had been participating in detestable practices, including gross violence, prostitution, and child sacrifices.

Other Old Testament examples that clearly show God's grace has limits can be found in the account of Noah and the ark in Genesis 6-9, and the destruction of Sodom and Gomorrah in

Genesis 18-19. With the exception of Noah and his family, the inhabitants of the earth had become corrupt beyond the point that their hearts would ever turn to God, so He sent a flood to destroy them. And the cities of Sodom and Gomorrah were totally destroyed along with their inhabitants because not even ten righteous people could be found there. Their opportunity to turn to God had come and gone because of a persistent choice to remain in their sin. Only Abraham's nephew Lot and his family were allowed to leave before the cities met with destruction.

In the bigger picture we know that the opportunity to accept God's gift of salvation, His son Jesus, will eventually come to an end. Those who choose to reject Him until death will be sent to hell, the place of eternal torment. This will no doubt come after God has introduced some type of tough love in each of their lives trying to prevent them from inflicting the ultimate destruction upon themselves. Yes God's grace is immense and immeasurable, but those who persist in taking it for granted will eventually find it does have a limit.

TAKING THE GRACE OF GOD FOR GRANTED

I mentioned the Apostle Paul briefly earlier in this chapter. We know him as the man who wrote most of the New Testament, laying the foundation for much of the doctrine we follow as Christians. But there was a time, when he was still known as Saul, that he was the foremost persecutor of Christians shortly after Jesus' crucifixion. Yet God had a plan for Paul, and he became a Christian himself after a dramatic encounter with the resurrected Jesus in a vision (Acts 9:4-9).

So Paul was a man who had an almost unprecedented understanding of the value and importance of grace. But his perspective was also properly balanced. After writing extensively about God's grace in Romans 5, he said in Romans 6:1-2: "What shall we say, then? Shall we go on sinning so that grace may increase? By no means! We died to sin; how can we live in it any longer?" Paul had no intention of taking the grace of God for granted. He lived that new life to the full — not for selfish gain, but for the sake of the Kingdom.

The author of the book of Jude, who was most likely a half-brother of Jesus, also warned against taking the grace of God for granted. He wrote in Jude 1:4: "For certain men whose condemnation was written about long ago have secretly slipped in among you. They are godless men, who change the grace of our God into a license for immorality and deny Jesus Christ our only Sovereign and Lord."

After reading this passage I felt an instant connection with Jude. He too felt a compelling need to warn fellow believers about the dangerous Kingdom invaders of his time.

GOD'S GRACE IS SUFFICIENT FOR YOU

Before I conclude this chapter I just want to make sure I'm not misunderstood. I don't want anyone to think that I am not fully aware of the importance of God's grace. Just as we can attempt to make God too *grace-full* so as to match our own beliefs, it would also be a mistake to make Him out to be too *grace-less*.

As I mentioned a little earlier, I spent many years falling short of what I should have been as a Christian. In the Frank Sinatra song "I Did It My Way" the iconic singer croons: "Regrets, I've had a few, yet still too few to mention." I wish I could say that. The fact is, looking back on my life I have way more regrets than I care to mention. But God extended his precious grace, patiently waiting for me to learn the lessons He was trying to teach me. When I didn't respond immediately, He pursued me and allowed serious heartache into my life to get my attention. When I finally was broken into repentance, God forgave me through His matchless grace and wrapped me in His unconditional love.

So if you think that God could never forgive you for what you've done in the past, you need not fear; His grace is sufficient for you. If you are afraid that God can't forgive you because of your current struggle with sin, you need not fear; His grace is sufficient for you. As long as your sincere desire is to please God with your life and you never give up trying, you need not fear; His grace is sufficient for you.

CONCLUDING THOUGHT

Let's face it, those who truly love God will not use His grace as an excuse to be self-serving in their faith, but rather, as a motivation to live sacrificially and faithfully for Him. John 14:21 says: "Whoever has my commands and obeys them, he is the one who loves me. He who loves me will be loved by my Father, and I too will love him and show myself to him."

I would encourage you to continually do a self-evaluation of your faith. Does the sin you see around you grieve your heart? Are you bothered by the sin you see in your own life? Do you have a desire to know God more and gain a greater understanding of His precepts? Does pleasing God in the way you live your life mean more to you than pleasing yourself?

These questions can act like a thermometer in taking your spiritual temperature. If the answer to any of them is "no" then you could be guilty of taking God's grace for granted. I would urge you to make every effort from this time on to show Him how much you appreciate Him and all He's done for you. Make God your priority over everything else by faithfully attending church services, spending time in daily Bible study and prayer, obeying His commands, and living out your faith in a way that represents Jesus Christ well — both at home and in public.

7–DANGEROUS DECEPTIONS: HETEROSEXUALITY

*There are certainly issues that can be considered "gray areas"
where sincere Christians disagree based on their interpretation
of Scripture. But there is simply no wiggle room when it comes
to God's design for marriage and sexuality.*

I'm going to begin the next two chapters with a little disclaimer. These are the only two chapters in an otherwise family-friendly book that have a PG-13 rating, for "parental guidance suggested for those under the age of 13." This is obviously because of the subject matter. A small amount of graphic language had to be used, but only as much as necessary to make important points and bring clarity. I trust as you read, you will see that I tried to use discretion. I've done my best to honor God in the way I have dealt with a difficult subject that simply has to be discussed. This is information that is critically important for young people to know, so I have tried to make it appropriate reading for anyone who has reached at least their teen years.

ONCE RESPECTED, NOW DETESTED

As a child growing up in the 1960's, I was treated to a wonderful array of family-friendly sitcoms. Among them were *Father Knows Best*, *Leave it to Beaver*, and *The Dick Van Dyke Show*. These shows portrayed loving, traditional families with wise fathers and caring mothers. Then there were sitcoms like *My*

Three Sons, *The Andy Griffith Show*, and *The Partridge Family*. In these shows we saw single parents raising their children in a loving environment. It should be pointed out that in each of these sitcoms the parents were not divorced, but rather, widowers or widows. There was also *The Brady Bunch* which showed a married couple with a blended family. And again, they had not been previously divorced, but had both lost their spouses to death.

Why do I feel it's important to point out the marital status of these parents? After all, I know these shows were only make believe and for the entertainment of the viewers. But there is significance in the fact that traditional families were regularly portrayed — and they were honored, not belittled. These sitcoms reflected that the biblical design for marriage and families at that time was still common and understood to be the healthiest way to raise children and maintain strong societies. In fact, according to government statistics from 1960, only about five percent of all U.S. births were to unmarried women.

The change since that time has been dramatic (both in sitcoms and real life). As of 2013, the National Marriage Project at the University of Virginia reported that the number of children born to unmarried mothers had grown to 48 percent! A major reason for this is the significant growth in couples who are cohabiting before they get married, if they get married at all. A report by the National Center for Health Statistics that same year found that more than half of U.S. women had lived with a boyfriend by the age of 25, and nearly 20 percent of these women became pregnant during their first year of cohabitation.

TOO MUCH OF THE MUSINGS OF MAN

There are certainly issues that can be considered "gray areas" where sincere Christians disagree based on their interpretation of Scripture. But there is simply no wiggle room when it comes to God's design for marriage and sexuality.

I remember back in 2009, a major mainline denomination released a forty-four page statement on human sexuality. When

I heard about this I thought, "How can it take forty-four pages to say 'sex is to be enjoyed only between one man and one woman within the confines of their own marriage?'"

But when I read the statement I realized it contained some messages with which I wholeheartedly agreed. It said there is no place for abuse in any kind of sexual or marital relationship. And they rebuked any disrespect or hatred toward anyone, regardless of their sexual orientation or perceived gender identity. This is important because we need to love all people, regardless of whether we agree with their lifestyle or not, as they too are beloved creations of God. But beyond that, I found way too much of the musings of man in the statement, and far too little of the direction of Scripture.

It seemed to me that the statement was an almost agonizing attempt on the part of the leadership of this denomination to somehow reconcile what man *wants* appropriate sexuality to be and what actually *is* appropriate in the eyes of God. The rambling statement spoke often about the virtues of love, trust, and commitment in relationships, and very little about honoring God by keeping his commandments regarding marriage and proper sexual expression. The things that influence sexual behavior, such as "social forces" and "the complexity of human relationships," were placed in higher regard than the timeless truths found in God's Word.

As evidenced by this denominational statement, misconceptions about what is appropriate sexuality are invading the Kingdom at an alarming rate today, and the subject has to be addressed. Nobody would want to be wrong about such a critical issue that may have eternal implications, including me. So I'm not going to base what I write in the next few pages based on mere tradition; it has to be about what the Bible says. As always, unless it is based on Scripture, anything we believe about anything is merely opinion.

TANTALIZING TEMPTATIONS

I talked to a man from this same mainline denomination who had apparently been influenced by the philosophies found in the statement. I'll call him Theodore. He asked me, "Isn't it unrealistic in this day and age to expect someone to abstain from sex until they are married?" There was certainly some merit to what he said. We live in such a hyper-sexualized society today that you can't walk down the street without seeing a tantalizing billboard, or watch a game on TV without seeing racy advertising, or turn on the computer without facing an onslaught of tempting messages and images.

If that isn't bad enough, we have plenty of flesh and blood temptations to deal with — even in our churches. I have seen some otherwise very godly young females wearing the shortest of shorts, skirts or dresses, and the tightest of pants. And ladies, please hear me. Even the smallest amount of exposed cleavage is tantalizing to the average male. No, we are not perverts. We have been designed by God to be visual creatures. You need to help us by dressing modestly. Add a few inches to those shorts, skirts or dresses. Get pants that are a slightly larger size. And cover that cleavage. It is unquestionably possible to dress modestly and fashionably at the same time.

One of the worst examples I can recall happened at a family Bible camp during an unusually hot Minnesota summer. Several young ladies were going to the beach in very small bikinis. Not only that, but they often walked through the camp that way, no doubt trying to stay cool in the heat. The problem was, they were increasing the "temperature" on a significant number of men who happened to get an inadvertent eyeful.

This type of thing is troubling on a couple of different levels. First of all, to the unsaved such immodesty reflects poorly on the God we represent. He is not honored when women flaunt that which is intended to create arousal only within their marriage. Secondly, women who dress that way can clearly cause a spiritually weak brother to stumble into lust; a case of sin breeding sin. That leads to my greatest concern about this issue.

You don't have to look very far to find a weaker brother. Perhaps you are aware of the polls showing that a significant percentage of self-professed Christians, and even pastors, have a problem with pornography. Who knows how many men from all walks of life come to our churches, Bible camps, or retreats looking for a blessed spiritual experience — maybe even seeking deliverance from sexual addictions — only to be faced with an onslaught of female flesh everywhere they look.

SEE AND FLEE

But guys, this doesn't give us an excuse for inappropriate responses to scantily-clad women. The world is fond of saying, "look, but don't touch." However, God calls us to a higher standard. He says, "see, but don't look." The look but don't touch philosophy is good when you're standing next to a classic car, but it is altogether insufficient when the object of your gaze is a well-built woman. We can't possibly avoid all of the tantalizing visual stimuli around us, but it is not acceptable to sit there and stare, soaking it all in as long as possible. When we do see someone that "pushes our buttons," we as Christians are expected to quickly look away, not dwelling on the source of temptation. This concept is spelled out well in the terrific 1987 Steven Curtis Chapman song "Run Away" (Sparrow Records):

> Strolling past Temptation Avenue
> You hear so many voices calling you
> Maybe you'll step in and take a quick look around
> But try to walk through it and you're gonna fall down
>
> You've gotta run away
> Turn around and run the other way
> Don't even look in the direction of a thought
> you should not entertain
> You gotta run away
> It's a prison that is calling your name

You just can't win if you play
So run away

We are continually instructed throughout the Bible to "run away" from temptation. In 1 Corinthians 6:18 we are told to flee "sexual immorality." In 1 Corinthians 10:14 we are instructed to flee idolatry. (By the way, sex has literally become an idol for many people. They use it as a temporary way of dealing with pain, depression, stress, etc. rather than bringing these needs to God.) In 1 Timothy 6:11 we are told to flee various evils and pursue lives of righteousness and godliness. And in 2 Timothy 2:22 we are instructed to flee "the evil desires of youth" and, again, pursue righteousness. These verses leave absolutely no room for dwelling on sexually appealing stimuli; we are to flee, or run away, as quickly as possible.

Jesus put the greatest perspective on the issue in Matthew 5:27-28 when He said: "You have heard that it was said, 'Do not commit adultery.' But I tell you that anyone who looks at a woman lustfully has already committed adultery with her in his heart." In other words, the "look, but don't touch" approach can actually be sinful. Our standard as Christians simply has to be higher.

CORRUPTED BY THE CULTURE

It's not a surprise that our young people today develop a skewed sense of what is appropriate sexuality. For most, they grow up being bombarded with the world's ideas about what is proper. Popular music, movies, and TV shows — beginning for the most part in the 1970's — have been depicting marriage as merely an optional place for sexual expression. In the decades since, things have deteriorated to the point that virtually every portrayal of sexual activity is between unmarried couples. And it is seen as common for couples to "go to bed together" almost immediately once their feelings for one another are revealed.

The impact of modern culture on our sexual sensibilities reminds me of the Hebrew patriarchs in the Old Testament. The practices of the pagan cultures around them began to invade the Kingdom of that time and polygamy was common. While this has often been used to dispute that marriage is only meant to be the union of one man and one woman, I would challenge you to look at the lives of these men and the consequences they faced.

Abraham, Jacob, David, and Solomon were among those who had multiple wives. They no doubt were enticed by the thought that sexual involvement with numerous women could be "legitimized" by taking them as wives and concubines. (Concubines were basically women who were slaves or captives. The patriarchs' sexual relationships with these women would likely be considered legitimized in their own minds by taking them as "common law" wives.)

While it may seem like these patriarchs had it made with their smorgasbord of lovers, the fact is that no sin goes unpunished. God's design for marriage is unambiguously presented in Genesis 2:22-24:

> Then the Lord God made a woman from the rib he had taken out of the man, and he brought her to the man. The man said, "This is now bone of my bones and flesh of my flesh; she shall be called woman, for she was taken out of man." For this reason a man will leave his father and mother and be united to his wife, and they will become one flesh.

The Hebrew word that is translated here in the NIV as "be united," or in the King James Version as "cleave," literally means "fused together." In other words, marriage is intended to be an unbreakable bond between the man and his wife. We can know for certain that this design was not meant just for Adam and Eve because, as the first people, they did not have any fathers or mothers to leave. No, marriage was created by God to be the union of one man and one woman for life — meant for all people for all time. Because the patriarchs did not follow this established plan for marriage and sexuality, they each suffered great consequences.

Abraham fathered Ishmael with Hagar, the maid of his wife Sarah. Because of Sarah's bitterness, Hagar and Ishmael were dismissed from the family, causing great anguish to Abraham. This polygamous relationship began turmoil that has lasted throughout history. Ishmael was the first of the Arab race. Genesis 16:12 says of Ishmael: "He will be a wild donkey of a man; his hand will be against everyone and everyone's hand will be against him, and he will live in hostility toward all his brothers."

We see this prophecy being fulfilled today in dramatic measure. Just as God's message to Abraham in Genesis 12 that he would be made into a great nation was meant to describe his descendents, so too this prophecy relating to Ishmael describes his family line. The vast majority of Ishmael's descendents, the Arab people, are Muslims today. In their desire to claim the entire world for Islam, a large number of Muslims — about 28 percent according to a 2014 Pew Research study — believe violent jihad (or Holy War) is acceptable to advance the will of their god, Allah.

This is being played out around the world in various acts of terror such as the infamous 9/11 attacks on the United States, a nation considered in Islam to be the "Great Satan." More recently, we are seeing non-Muslims being threatened in various Muslim-majority countries with heavy taxation, imprisonment, or even death if they refuse to convert. (By the way, these actions against "infidels" are actually condoned in the Qur'an, the Islamic "holy book," in surahs 9:29 and 5:33 among others.)

Violence between the different Muslims sects, primarily Sunni and Shiite, has also taken on more intensity and barbarity in recent days. In other words, there is hostility toward their own Islamic brothers — again in fulfillment of biblical prophecy. (We will look at the religion of Islam in greater detail in chapter nine.)

The polygamy of Abraham's grandson, Jacob, led to great contention in the house between his wives Rachel and Leah, who were sisters. Rachel, Jacob's favorite, had difficulty bearing children. So when she finally did conceive, her son Joseph was favored by Jacob above his sons birthed by Leah. This led to jealousy among Joseph's half-brothers who ended up selling him into slavery. From that time on Jacob suffered painful heartache. Because of lies told to him by his other sons, Jacob lived out most of his life believing his beloved Joseph was dead.

King David's sin with Bathsheba, in which he eventually took her as one of his wives, led to a tremendous amount of discord and tragedy in his house. Their first child died as a newborn, bringing great anguish to David. Later, David's daughter Tamar was raped by her half-brother, Amnon. In revenge, David's son Absalom (and Tamar's full-brother) killed Amnon. After this, Absalom fled and 2 Samuel 13:27 says David "mourned for his son every day." Several years later, Absalom conspired to kill his father and steal his throne. Absalom ended up being killed as an enemy of the king and David suffered even more heartache. Significant portions of the book of Psalms were written by David, expressing his grief and sorrow at his sin and subsequent consequences.

Solomon, a son of David and Bathsheba, had his own problems because of polygamy. According to 1 Kings 11, Solomon had a thousand wives altogether. Although a Godly man early in his life, Solomon's many wives ended up turning his heart away from the Lord and he suffered greatly because of this. Solomon spent a significant part of his life in a "meaningless" pursuit of happiness and pleasure. His years of discouragement and depression are chronicled in the book of Ecclesiastes which he wrote late in his life after learning the "folly" of trying to live a fulfilled life apart from God.

We can see a similarity to these patriarchs today in that many who would call themselves Christians are being dramatically influenced by the culture around them. While polygamy is rare, many are still acting out sexually in ways that grieve the Lord. Sadly, a significant number are having sexual relations with their boyfriend or girlfriend before marriage. Many are cohabiting with their partners, which in a purer time was understood to be "living in sin." And more recently, some who would consider themselves to be Christians are participating in homosexual relationships, and even "marrying" their same-sex partners where it is legal.

SELFISH SEXUALITY

There have been many couples involved in premarital sex or extra-marital affairs who have believed their love was so true and so beautiful that it simply must be condoned by God; that somehow the rules don't apply to them. But this would be like a song that grabs your heart with its beautiful and emotional music, yet is tainted with immoral lyrics. One example that comes to mind is the 1979 song "Sad Eyes" (EMI) by Robert John:

> Looks like it's over, you knew I couldn't stay
> She's coming home today
> We had a good thing, I'll miss your sweet love
> Why must you look at me that way?
> It's over
>
> Sad eyes, turn the other way
> I don't want to see you cry
> Sad eyes, you knew there'd come a day
> When we would have to say "goodbye"
>
> Try to remember the magic that we shared
> In time your broken heart will mend
> I never used you, you knew I really cared
> I hate to see it have to end
> But it's over

As a kid, I thought this was such a beautiful song focused on the heartbreaking end of a truly loving relationship. But in recent years, as the Holy Spirit has continued his work of sanctification and made me more sensitive to sin, this song has revealed itself for what it is.

The man had made a previous commitment to another woman (whether married or not we don't know) but he is cheating on her while she is away. To his mistress he declares, "I never used you, you knew I really cared." But I beg to differ. He knew this side relationship was only temporary, so he was selfishly using this woman until his "real" lover returned. In reality, there is nothing beautiful about this at all.

Paul wrote in 1 Thessalonians 4:3-6:

It is God's will that you should be sanctified: that you should avoid sexual immorality; that each of you should learn to control his own body in a way that is holy and honorable, not in passionate lust like the heathen, who do not know God; and that in this matter no one should wrong his brother or take advantage of him.

So according to this passage of Scripture, immoral relationships that seem beautiful and loving are, at their roots, usually driven by selfishness. They are wronging another, or taking advantage of them.

For those who are not married, a sexual relationship with another creates a bond that is much more painful upon a break-up. And it is often very painful to a future spouse. This kind of baggage brought into a marriage can be destructive on many levels. First, knowing the intimacy shared with another can be an emotionally devastating discovery for the spouse. Second, the opportunity for comparison in the bedroom can be a significant hindrance to a healthy, fulfilling sexual relationship for the married couple. In a sense, the memories mean they are never really alone in bed. And third, there is the potential of introducing a sexually-transmitted disease into the marriage from any past relationship.

While most unmarried sexual relationships are driven by self-ishness, I realize not all of them are. Some are prompted by factors such as pain or fear. I was talking with a man recently, I'll call him Darren, who said he had been living with his girlfriend for ten years. I hadn't known Darren for very long when we began our discussion so I didn't feel comfortable asking him why he and his girlfriend had never gotten married. But it became pretty obvious when certain details were revealed.

Darren said his girlfriend had been previously married and had two children from that relationship. After a decade together he said those kids considered him to be their dad, particularly because their biological father didn't really have much to do with them.

Darren also talked about his own parents and what he saw in their marriage while growing up. He said their relationship had always been rocky and that they should have gotten divorced twenty years ago. But since they didn't believe in divorce they have remained together.

Putting two and two together, it was easy to see why Darren and his girlfriend had chosen to avoid getting married. She had already been through the devastating pain of divorce and wanted to avoid the possibility of facing that again. After observing his parents, Darren feared making a vow to remain with someone who could end up causing him a lifetime of unhappiness.

It was clear to me that Darren was a comparatively honorable man. He had willingly taken on the tough responsibility of caring for his girlfriend and helping her raise her kids. He gave no indication of any problems with their long-term live-in relationship, but there are inevitably consequences when God's design for sexual expression is not followed.

Regardless, making decisions prompted by pain or fear is rarely a good thing. Satan is the author of pain and fear and he regularly uses them to cloud our reasoning. This often leads very rational people to make very irrational decisions, whether they are otherwise driven by selfishness or not.

For married individuals who are having an affair, the implications of selfishness should be obvious. It is the ultimate betrayal, in which there is no thought given to the pain being caused to the spouse or their children. STD's are also a potential problem for the victimized spouse.

In any scenario, there is nothing beautiful about the shame brought to the reputation of Jesus when those who call themselves Christians participate in immoral behavior. These relationships grieve the heart of God. And there are few things I can think of that are more selfish than living for our own pleasure while friends and loved ones who see our hypocritical example tumble toward an eternity in hell.

REMORSE AND REWARD

Whether consciously or unconsciously, the actions of some people are driven by the belief that since the Bible says none of us are perfect and we're all going to sin anyway we might as well sin in the most enjoyable way possible. But no matter what the lie of Satan may be at the time, there is no immoral relationship that is ultimately worth the consequences. Just as with the patriarchs no sin goes unpunished forever, and pain and regret are the common result. As it says in 1 Thessalonians 4:6-7: "The Lord will punish men for all such sins, as we have already told you and warned you. For God did not call us to be impure, but to live a holy life."

There are literally millions of people throughout history who have been devastated emotionally and/or physically because of their sexual transgressions. The repercussions sometimes can be less obvious to the point that only God knows if they correlate to the sexual sin, such as ill health in the children born through these relationships, or a painful divorce after many years of marriage.

When I was a child, there was a couple I knew that was in ministry together. I'll call them Frank and Laura. About twenty years later when I was an adult I was informed of the stunning news that Laura had left Frank for another man. Of course, Frank was heartbroken. But he continued to trust in the Lord and remained faithful to Him through his painful trial.

Fast forward another twenty years and an interesting thing happened. I ran into Laura before a church service at a time when she was trying to get her life back on track with the Lord. I didn't recognize her at first but I told her she looked familiar. Laura was still with the man for whom she had left Frank, but it quickly became obvious that her actions from two decades earlier were still haunting her. When she realized I knew her from her past ministry, Laura started to cry as I became an instant reminder of what she had done. I told her I was not there to judge and that the Lord can forgive her. Unfortunately, I never saw Laura again and my last memory of her was the anguished tears of remorse rolling down her face.

Then, within just a couple of months, I ran into Frank as well. He was with a beautiful new wife (such a remarriage is understood by most theologians to be acceptable in the case of adultery or abandonment) and I had rarely seen such a happy, fulfilled person. It was clear to me that the choice Frank had made so many years ago to honor God in the midst of his pain was in turn being rewarded. He and his wife were in ministry together and his life had begun again.

This scenario plays out time after time. When we choose obedience to God with our sexuality, the reward is ultimately great. When we choose disobedience, there may be joy in the sin for a season, but regret is never far away.

THERE IS A PRICE TO PAY

I have been trying to lose 20 to 25 pounds for more than four years. I've known that being overweight is not healthy for my body, which of course, is the temple of the Holy Spirit. (As a friend of mine once said: "If I had known my body was a temple I wouldn't have treated it like an amusement park!") I have already shared with you my love of sweets. I also have a passion for buffets — it's not just a meal to me, it's entertainment — so losing weight obviously is an uphill battle.

Recently, I've noticed some pain in my lower back and hips just from taking my usual daily walks. I am beginning to experience physically what I already knew mentally — you can't continue living in ways that are unhealthy forever without repercussions. The same can be said for sexual sin. You can go on for a long time thinking that you're getting away with the sinful behavior without consequence, but eventually there is a price to pay.

A HIGHER STANDARD

Back in the 1990's, President Bill Clinton was caught in an adulterous relationship with an intern. When word of their White House rendezvous leaked out, Clinton told Congress and the American people that he did not have sexual relations with the intern, but it was later revealed that they indeed had participated in an intimate relationship. Clinton reasoned that he really didn't lie, because their intimacy didn't include actual intercourse. Unfortunately, that reasoning was bought into by a significant number of young people at the time, as has crept into the thinking of many of our Christian youth as well.

The mindset is largely, "as long as we don't go all the way then playing around is not a sin." But the Greek word that is translated as "fornication" in the King James Bible, and "sexual immorality" in the NIV and NASB, is "porneia." The expanded definition of this word encompasses more than just sex outside of marriage. It also includes merely touching the intimate parts of another person's body, or even viewing the nakedness of another. This makes sense, because porneia is the root of our English word pornography.

I don't want to rush past this point too quickly. If viewing pornography for sexual gratification is clearly a sin, then why would it be acceptable in any way to view the nakedness of a flesh and blood person in our presence? And if just seeing the nakedness of another is sinful, then why would we believe touching their bodies would somehow be all right? With these things in mind it would be absolutely absurd to consider total intimacy outside of marriage to be in any way acceptable in the eyes of God.

REBOOTING RELATIONSHIPS

Remember when Theodore asked me, "Isn't it unrealistic in this day and age to expect someone to abstain from sex until they are married?" Well, it certainly is unrealistic if we believe everything short of intercourse is acceptable behavior. Sadly, many couples have become fully aware that even if you want to wait until you get married to have sex, you aren't going to make it if you are hanging around "Temptation Avenue." We need to totally "reboot" how we go about our dating relationships as Christians or we will continue to fall short of what God requires.

When Theodore asked me that question, I felt I had to find for him an example of a couple who was able to forsake the cultural tide and remain sexually pure until marriage. It didn't take long. Within the previous few months I had attended the wedding of a godly young couple who had served as youth leaders at our church. I said to the man, "I'm sure I already know the answer to this question, but I just have to ask you: Did you and your new bride abstain from sex until you were married?"

His answer was pleasantly surprising. He said, "Not only did we refrain from sex, but the first time we kissed was on the platform at the end of our wedding ceremony." He went on to share with me an instruction that is repeated no less than three times in the romantic Old Testament book, the Song of Songs (traditionally known as Song of Solomon). In 2:7, 3:5, and 8:4 is the commandment this man lived by in his dating relationships: "Do not arouse or awaken love until it so desires."

Put into context, this passage is unquestionably talking about sexuality. Now this concept may sound quite extreme in today's permissive culture, but it is really loaded with common sense. Dennis Rainey, founder of the Family Life ministry, is among those who endorse waiting for that first kiss until the wedding day. He reasons that anything unmarried romantic partners do that causes sexual arousal should be immediately stopped because it cannot be satisfied in a godly way. So if kissing causes arousal, then it shouldn't happen. Even if holding hands causes arousal, it should be stopped.

When you think about it, this isn't some kind of puritanical pretense — it is actually the essence of common sense. And it bears repeating: anything unmarried romantic partners do that causes sexual arousal should be immediately stopped because it cannot be satisfied in a godly way.

Right about now you may be rolling your eyes and muttering to yourself, "This is ridiculous." But as I said earlier we need to totally "reboot" how we go about our dating relationships as Christians or we will continue to grieve the heart of God, routinely falling short of what He requires. As Paul wrote in 1 Thessalonians 4:8 in relation to sexual sin: "Therefore, he who rejects this instruction does not reject man but God, who gives you his Holy Spirit."

THE PORN PERSPECTIVE

Before we move on, I want to expound on the issue of pornography. I said earlier that viewing porn for sexual gratification is clearly a sin. Sadly, even that statement has come into question with some who would call themselves Christians in our postmodern age. A couple of verses we looked at earlier really put a great perspective on this issue as well. Jesus said in Matthew 5:27-28: "You have heard that it was said, 'Do not commit adultery.' But I tell you that anyone looks at a woman lustfully has already committed adultery with her in his heart." Even if you are not married, the argument can be made that you are still committing adultery when viewing porn because you are lusting after a woman who is not your future wife.

Pornography is not a "victimless" crime as some would lead you to believe. No real-life woman could ever live up to the airbrushed perfection of pornographic images, leaving every wife to compete for her husband's sexual desire against unrealistic standards. And many a wife has been devastated to learn of her husband's consumption of pornography. As a man I can only imagine what a blow that would be to a woman's self-esteem. What a painful betrayal to know that a husband is gratifying his sexual desires in such a vile way. But the problem goes way beyond the intangible of mere feelings or emotion.

Perhaps you've noticed the many commercials these days for erectile dysfunction drugs. There is a direct correlation between the epidemic of ED and the exponential increase in the use of pornography thanks to the internet. Excessive viewing of porn actually has the affect of "warping" the pleasure center of the brain so that a person has difficulty getting aroused by the real thing. This clearly creates a problem whether you're married or not. In marriage, it obviously affects the sexual relationship with one's spouse. For those who are not married, it begins a dysfunction that likely will last into marriage and could hinder their sexual pleasure the rest of their lives.

In more extreme cases, the effects of excessive pornography consumption can be horrifying. Left unabated, there is a common progression that takes place in the life of a porn addict. As his brain gets warped, he needs to seek more perverse images to get the same sexual "high." This perversion often includes children or depictions of violence. Eventually, the images are not enough to fulfill their desires and the porn addict will seek to turn them into reality. He will then act out with real people, with or without their consent. It is no coincidence that the number of abductions and the unimaginable scourge of sex trafficking has skyrocketed in this age of easily-available internet porn.

And don't be fooled by the use of the word "erotica." This term is commonly used to describe pornographic images or acts that supposedly aren't demeaning. The argument is that the human body is artistically beautiful, and subjects engaging in erotica are expressing a respectful form of sexuality. But let's face it, this is an evil smokescreen. No matter how "intellectual" the argument, anyone who wants to be honest would have to admit that — with very rare exception — the reason for viewing nudity in images or activity is to gain sexual arousal.

With a biblical understanding of the sinful human nature, it doesn't take a genius to know that erotica opens the door for Satan and his cronies to go to work. Just as marijuana is often a first step on the path to a dangerous drug addiction, so erotica is often a first step in the progression toward more graphic forms of pornography. And as I said earlier, the Bible makes it clear that viewing the nakedness of anyone apart from your spouse is sexual immorality, whether the images or acts are considered demeaning or not. In Psalm 101:3, as David was recommitting himself to the Lord after his grievous sexual sin, he wrote, "I will set before my eyes no vile thing." That needs to be our resolve as well if we are truly committed followers of Jesus Christ.

Women aren't completely insulated from similar types of addictions. While they are generally not as captivated by visual images, women are often drawn to "emotional porn" such as romance novels. Many contain very graphic and tantalizing language which is clearly sinful. But even so-called "Christian" romance novels have been known to have a negative impact. Although they contain purer thoughts and language, women can still find themselves getting wrapped up in the strong, yet sensitive men found in these books.

In a parallel to visual pornography, women who become obsessed with emotional porn can inadvertently become dissatisfied with their marital relationships, or feed the discontent that may already exist. Real-life husbands simply can't measure up to the "air-brushed" perfection of the men in the novels and many of these women have admittedly been tempted to seek out adulterous relationships.

THE CONSEQUENCES OF COHABITATION

With all I've already shared about the sinfulness of sex outside of marriage, it wouldn't seem necessary to talk about whether or not it is acceptable for unmarried Christian couples to live together. But Satan has a way of convincing people of things that simply aren't true, and with something as pleasurable as sex even Christians seem to be especially vulnerable to deception. It's a cultural lie, and ultimately a satanic lie, to say that it is OK for committed couples to live together outside of marriage.

Beware of those who say that, in their experience, living together outside of marriage has been a good thing. Because I have heard couples from every perspective offering justification for their choice to cohabit:

- If they lived together but then split up before marriage, then cohabiting was good because the relationship ended without the complications of divorce.

- If they lived together but then split up after getting married, then it was the marriage that ruined their relationship so they should have just continued to cohabit.

- If they lived together and later ended up having a successful marriage, then cohabiting first was wise because they were able to learn that they would be compatible once they got married.

- If they lived and stayed together without ever getting married, then it was proof that marriage was not necessary for their relationship to succeed.

So if someone tries to deceive you into believing that living together before marriage is a good thing, don't fall for it. People can convince themselves of just about anything if they want to believe it bad enough.

They also may try to convince you of just about anything. I have talked with more than one person who claimed a commitment to Christ, while at the same time living with their romantic partner. They said they didn't sleep in the same room so what they were doing was OK. Of course, they were implying that living together and having a sexual relationship wasn't necessarily the same thing. But when I pressed them for the truth, to a person they admitted that their relationship was sexually intimate. You simply can't step into "Temptation Avenue" and not expect to fall. Even if it were possible to remain celibate in such a situation, there would still be the appearance of evil seen by unsaved neighbors, friends, and loved ones which condones a behavior contrary to God's design.

But for most cohabiting couples, they don't try to hide that they're living as if married. The thought process is, "you test drive a car before you buy it, so why wouldn't you test out a prospective spouse first?" But the success rate for marriages that follow live-in relationships is actually very poor. Depending on the study, statistics show that couples who cohabit before getting married are anywhere from 50 to 100 percent more likely to get a divorce than those who don't live together first. Look at those numbers again. Divorce is not just a little bit more likely for previously cohabiting couples, it is *significantly* more likely. Why is that?

God knows how He made us and how we think. He knows that when marriage is not honored as the exclusive place for sexual intimacy it has an impact on our mentality. There are elements of selfishness, insecurity, lack of trust, and questions of commitment that can either consciously or unconsciously invade the mindset of those who choose to live together. These dynamics all have an impact on their relationship over time, whether the couple ends up getting married or not. Perhaps even more significant, there is an element of rebellion against God that cannot help but put the relationship at risk. Disobedience to His commands opens the door wide for Satan to wreak havoc in their lives, whether immediately or years down the road.

There are also consequences for the children that come from a cohabiting relationship. Certainly exceptions exist, but overall children have a greater sense of security when their parents express their commitment to one another through marriage. A host of studies have also shown that life outcomes are far better for children raised in homes with a married father and mother. They are less likely to get in trouble in school, less likely to get pregnant in their teens, less likely to end up incarcerated at some point in their lives, and less likely to end up in poverty. The statistics leave no doubt that God's design for families is what's best for parents, their kids, and society as a whole.

CONCLUDING THOUGHT

God made sex to be something very special that is not to be enjoyed temporarily until a relationship ends, and then shared with another and another until Mr. or Ms. Right is found. It is designed to be a union between only one man and one woman for life in the context of marriage.

In some remarkable evidences of this truth, the bodies of a couple that has regular sexual activity exclusively with each other — such as in a healthy marital relationship — actually adapt to one another so the woman in particular is protected from any potential infections or diseases through their union. And in recent years, it has been discovered that there is a hormonal reaction that occurs in the body during sexual activity that causes a person to emotionally and physically desire a return to that "place."

Put another way, it creates a mental *and* physiological bonding between the couple; they become in a very real sense "one flesh" just as described in Genesis 2:24! With this understanding, it should be clear that sex was designed by God to be an exclusive, special bond meant only for a married couple until death parts them.

8–DANGEROUS DECEPTIONS: HOMOSEXUALITY

God is the One who knows what sin is and what grieves His heart; we cannot write our own rules about what is right and wrong. And the Lord is neither silent nor ambivalent on this issue.

I'm going to transition now to a subject that has become a major hot-button issue, not just in the culture, but in many of our churches. Homosexuality was once understood by Christians, and society at large, to be a deviation from the proper expression of sexuality. But popular forms of entertainment have been among the tools effectively used by those seeking to advance the gay rights agenda. Homosexual behavior is regularly depicted in media such as TV and movies as absolutely normal, and anybody who questions this is made to look pathetically ridiculous. This has contributed to the rapid shift in the way our culture views homosexuality today.

God's timing is so perfect. It was remarkable to me that as I was preparing to write this chapter, one of the few modern TV shows I still enjoyed watching had a very pro-gay episode. In it, those who favored homosexuality as a legitimate lifestyle were portrayed as thoughtful, sensitive, caring, and in every way rational and reasonable. Those who opposed the full acceptance of homosexual behavior were made to look hateful, ignorant, and completely out of touch.

Among those who spoke in favor of homosexuality during this episode were a well-known, highly-esteemed Catholic man and a nun who was secretly lesbian. The carefully scripted, pro-gay dialogue regularly discussed the Catholic Church and its "archaic" doctrines and how it needs to change with the times. Not once was the Bible mentioned. Of course, what we believe on this or any other issue cannot be based on man's beliefs or even church doctrine. Everything we stand for has to be founded on the timeless truths contained in God's Word.

SILENCE IS NOT GOLDEN

That episode was reflective of the cultural battle we now face when taking a biblical stand on this important issue. In the not-too-distant past, the number of people who considered themselves to be homosexual was so miniscule that it was easy to disparagingly characterize them as freaks and perverts. Unfortunately, many Christians were among those who treated them in that ungodly way which has given us a larger battle to overcome today.

As with the other forms of immoral sexual behavior, homosexuality has become more common in recent years. As it is gaining acceptance in the culture, Christians who would dare characterize homosexual activity as sinful are regularly being called "homophobic" and "haters." Those names may have been somewhat appropriate in the past, considering the way some believers treated those with same-sex attractions. And even today there are those who are doing us no favors through their venomous and hurtful attacks. But speaking the truth in love as Jesus requires is not hateful. And right now I am going to take a stand and say that based on what the Bible says, homosexual activity is sinful. However, I am *not* homophobic nor a hater.

On the contrary. The easiest thing people like me could do if we truly were afraid of or hated those who practice homosexuality would be to say nothing. If we were afraid of them, then saying nothing would allow us to live our lives quietly without any attacks or ridicule. If we hated them, then our silence would assure they would remain in their sin and end up in hell someday with all of the other unrepentant sinners — and we wouldn't care.

No, we speak out because God has given us a love in our hearts for these people. Those who advocate for homosexuality have a hard time processing how you can completely disagree with somebody's lifestyle and yet truly love them (1 Corinthians 2:14). But with the help of the Holy Spirit, followers of Jesus can see those who practice homosexuality as they really are — living in a prison created by a satanic deception. This is a strong statement to be sure. But those who have lived the gay lifestyle and "escaped" would characterize it that way. And there are literally thousands upon thousands who have done just that — escaped through the love and power of Jesus Christ.

THE MOST DESTRUCTIVE BELIEF

The fact that so many people have put that lifestyle behind them and are living free of same-sex attractions should put to rest the most destructive belief relating to homosexuality — that people are born that way. This is the first perception that has to be addressed when dealing with this issue. Because if you believe they are born that way and are homosexual through no choice of their own, then naturally, accepting their lifestyle is the most loving thing you can do.

That would explain why many friends and relatives of those with same-sex attractions become staunch advocates for homosexual rights, or why some denominations would choose to bless same-sex unions and ordain practicing gay clergy. Because if homosexuality is defined by what they *are* as opposed to what they *do*, then certainly we would want to give them every relational and marital right that heterosexuals have.

This too is why gay activists have characterized it as a civil rights issue instead of a moral issue. It is often compared to the struggle for civil rights among black people in the 1960's. But there are inescapable differences between the two. The most important is that black people *are* black people. They cannot change what they are anymore than white people, Asian people, Latino people, or any other kind of people can change what they are. The only things that change the number of people who are a part of any of these groups are the birth and death rates. This is not the case with those who practice homosexuality.

As I mentioned earlier, the number of people who forsake homosexuality and successfully overcome same-sex attractions is significant. It's very difficult to put a hard and fast number on these types of things because there are so many variables, including confidentiality issues and the potential for skewed statistics in order to advocate for one position or the other. But based on several studies of identical twins from 2000 to 2012 (which we will look at in more detail in a moment), about 3 percent of current heterosexuals at one time considered themselves to be homosexual or bisexual. So it is clear that a substantial number of people are experimenting with and changing their sexual identity at any given time.

A SCIENTIFIC EXAMINATION

Despite numerous attempts, there has never been a scientifically verifiable study ever done that shows any genetic, hormonal, or physical difference between heterosexuals and homosexuals. Much press has been given over the last couple of decades to any research that supposedly reveals evidence of gay genetics. But when this research is found to be inconclusive at best, or fraudulent at worst, this important new information does not receive nearly as much publicity and the damage has already been done. Because of this, many people today believe that homosexuality is genetic despite the lack of any legitimate proof.

Probably the strongest case against this belief can be found in the answer to a simple question: If people with same-sex attractions are born that way, then how do the gay genes get passed on? For this to happen, homosexuals would have to bear children. Since two people of the same gender can't procreate, a partner of the opposite sex would have to be involved for a pregnancy to occur. Even if something like artificial insemination was widespread, it still wouldn't explain why the number of people who practice homosexuality continues to grow. On the contrary, those with same-sex attractions would eventually become extinct.

With this common sense understanding, the gay gene theory has no basis in reality. And unlike the gay gene theory, the common sense understanding has plenty of scientific support. For example, no less than eight major studies of identical twins in three different countries have eliminated any credibility to the claim that homosexuality is genetic. Dr. Neil and Briar Whitehead are authors of the book *My Genes Made Me Do It*, a scientific look at sexual orientation covering 20 years of research. In their discussion of the twin studies, the Whiteheads note that identical twins share the same genes or DNA, so the findings are conclusive:

> "These very complex comparisons of identical twins and non-identical twins definitively rule out genetic determinism. Identical twins with identical genes are about 11-14% concordant for SSA [same-sex attractions]. If homosexuality were 'genetic,' identical co-twins of homosexual men and women would also be homosexual 100% of the time."[9]

Therefore, they say unwaveringly that no one is born gay. Rather, post-birth factors such as "individualistic reactions to chance events," including exposure to pornography or sexual abuse, "are by far the strongest contributors to homosexuality."

A SPIRITUAL EXAMINATION

Perhaps the strongest spiritual case against the belief that people are born gay is found in 1 Corinthians 6:9-10, where those who practice homosexuality are included with those who will not "inherit the Kingdom of God." In other words, they will not spend their eternity in the heavenly home Jesus is preparing for true believers (John 14:2). In keeping with His perfect, loving nature, God would never create a class of people who are destined for hell simply by being what He made them to be. That just wouldn't make any sense. If people are born homosexual, then they have no hope of salvation. This would be a direct contradiction to the unchangeable attribute of God that requires perfect justice.

But as this passage in 1 Corinthians continues, the hope is evident for "homosexual offenders," as well as all of the people caught up in sinful lifestyles. Verse 11 says, "And that is what some of you were." *Were* is past tense, meaning that the people Paul was writing to were able to overcome and turn from their sin. If those who practice homosexuality were born that way, this would be an impossibility.

There are many organizations that help people overcome same-sex attractions — including One by One, PFOX, and Pure Intimacy — that testify to this fact. Groups such as these are regularly founded and operated by those who formerly practiced homosexuality but are now set free, so they know how to provide the needed help without judgment or condemnation.

THE SPIRITUAL COMPONENT IS NON-NEGOTIABLE

The number of people who continue to be or become practicing homosexuals is hard to pin down for the same reasons listed previously. I have seen the percentage as low as 1 percent by those advocating for a traditional view of sexuality, to as high as 20 or 25 percent by gay rights advocates. But according to a review conducted by the Williams Institute in April 2011, about 1.7 percent of American adults classified themselves as either gay or lesbian, another 1.8 percent said they were bisexual, and 0.3 percent described themselves as transgender. So according to this study, the total number of U.S. citizens claiming to practice non-traditional sexuality would be about 3.8 percent.

This is a very small number to be able to wield so much power in the courts, legislatures, Congress, and more recently, in the hearts and minds of the average citizen. But as I said earlier, you can understand psychologically why support for homosexuals would become almost militant.

The media today glorifies homosexual behavior and vilifies anyone who disagrees. Over time, this "peer pressure" has had a powerful impact. And for those who care deeply about a friend or relative who says they are homosexual, once you take the spiritual component out of the picture, then acknowledging their lifestyle becomes a way of showing loving affirmation. All that's standing in the way is those of us who hold to a so-called narrow-minded, antiquated, and even hateful belief system.

But just as with everything else, we *can't* take the spiritual component out of it. God is the One who knows what sin is and what grieves His heart; we cannot write our own rules about what is right and wrong. And the Lord is neither silent nor ambivalent on this issue.

In the Old Testament, homosexual activity is clearly considered to be blatant sin in the eyes of God. The first example is in the cities of Sodom and Gomorrah in Genesis 19. God destroyed these two cities supernaturally with burning sulfur from the skies because of their grievous sin. I have heard various quasi-explanations for why Sodom and Gomorrah were destroyed, but homosexuality is the only obvious sin directly mentioned in Scripture relating to their residents. We even get our centuries-old English word sodomy, which describes homosexual acts, from one of these ill-fated cities.

Depending upon the translation, Leviticus 18:22 calls homosexual sex "detestable" or "an abomination." Keep in mind, there are many ceremonial and sacrificial laws the Old Testament Hebrews were instructed to follow that no longer apply to us under the New Covenant through Jesus Christ. But the moral laws relating to sex and other activities remain binding on us today, evidenced by the fact that they are reiterated in the New Testament.

In Romans 1:24-28, Paul writes of a people that "exchanged the truth of God for a lie." He says, "God gave them over to shameful lusts," which Paul describes as homosexual relationships, and these people "received in themselves the due penalty for their perversion." In verse 28, he writes again that God "gave them over to a depraved mind, to do what ought not to be done."

This reminds me once more of the Old Testament patriarchs. God gave them over to their "depraved minds" and allowed them to practice polygamy, which as we saw in the last chapter led to great hardship for them. The people of Paul's time were also given over to their depravity and suffered the consequences for their sinfulness. Today, we appear to be facing a similar situation and the question for Christians is, "what are we going to do about it?" At the end of Romans 1, verse 32 says: "Although they knew God's righteous decree that those who do such things deserve death, they not only continue to do these very things but also approve of those who practice them."

For clarification, this verse is talking about a number of different sins committed by the people of that culture, of which homosexual behavior is included. For further clarification, Paul is not advocating physical death for these people, but rather, is talking about the spiritual death that leads to an eternity in hell. With this in mind, we as Christians cannot be found guilty of giving our stamp of approval to homosexuality. If we do, the consequences will ultimately be great for them, for us, and for society as a whole.

A NUTS AND BOLTS REALITY

There is a particular phrase in this passage that I want to address in more detail before we move on. In the New American Standard Version of the Bible, Romans 1:26-27 says:

> ...for their women exchanged the natural function for that which is unnatural, and in the same way also the men abandoned the natural function of the woman and burned in their desire toward one another...

Consider the nut and bolt for a moment. They were created many years ago by a designer to have a natural function; one works in harmony with the other to achieve a productive purpose.

What happens when you try to put two bolts together, or try to make the nuts work without the bolts? They are removed from their natural function and their purpose cannot be achieved as created.

I'm sure you're already getting the point of this analogy. Let's face it, all it takes is one look at our anatomy as males and females to see who we are designed to mate with. If two men are together, or two women are together, they simply cannot fulfill the purpose which the creator, God, designed for them.

While we are on the subject of a creator, there is a topic for which the subject matter may have been more suited to the second chapter of this book relating to creation and evolution. But because it is of a more graphic nature, I decided to add it to our discussion about sexuality since a disclaimer has already been given. For those who question whether or not God exists, do you really think that wonderful feeling during orgasm could have just happened as part of an evolutionary process? It stretches beyond the scope of any rational thought to believe there was no intelligent, loving creator behind something so emotionally and physically captivating and fulfilling.

The rest of the biology surrounding sexuality points just as obviously to a master designer. The woman produces an egg. The male produces sperm. Through the union of their compatibly designed bodies, the sperm fertilizes the egg. The fertilized egg implants on the woman's uterine wall and a human begins its life. This new baby continues to get all it needs from inside its mommy for nine months until it is born. Even then, the woman has breasts which provide nutritious milk for the baby for several months after the birth. This design is unmistakable.

From start to finish, there are unquestionably natural functions for men and women that only work as designed by the creator, God himself. Anything other than one man with one woman for life is a deviation from His plan.

USING THE PAST TO STEAL THE FUTURE

The Bible tells us that everybody is born with a sinful nature. Looking at the situation from a spirit-realm perspective, I believe Satan assigns demons to study each person from the time they are born so these dark messengers can learn where people are most vulnerable. They are basically spies who provide the "inside information" needed to succeed in tempting each person at their weakest points.

Extensive studies have revealed that there are some common threads woven into the backgrounds of those who practice homosexuality. Sadly, these threads regularly include some type of painful or even traumatic experience such as growing up with a neglectful and/or abusive parent, or having been sexually molested — often by someone of the same gender. So when Satan knows that a person has been hurt in one of these ways, he will attack them, using their painful past against them in an attempt to steal their future. Seeds of deceptive temptation are planted in fertile soil, convincing this person that an intimate relationship with someone of the same gender is a safe place to find healing.

There are also many boys who are small or effeminate that get mercilessly teased which can devastate the fragile psyche of a young male. When boys do not feel like they measure up to the masculine ideal they can start questioning their own "maleness." Similarly, girls who exhibit a more prominent amount of masculinity can face similar amounts of painful teasing and begin to question their sexuality. This explains, at least in part, why some men who turn to homosexuality have distinctly feminine traits and some women are noticeably masculine. (Just for reference, I have known very effeminate men and very masculine women who had absolutely no inclination toward homosexuality.)

This phenomenon, by the way, can also play a role in transgender feelings where a person begins to believe they were born the wrong sex. Although the causes of transgenderism are varied, many of these people have gone through similar painful experiences which makes them vulnerable to satanic attack. We need to have great compassion on them as they have often suffered much in their lives.

It should be pointed out that, because we live in a sin-sick world, occasionally babies are born that develop certain sexual anomalies. For example, a chromosomal abnormality in males causes a disorder called Klinefelter Syndrome. Those who are born with this affliction have unusually small testicles. Because of this, they produce less of the male hormone testosterone. This leads to certain less-than-masculine physical traits such as enlarged breasts, reduced facial and body hair, an unusually small penis, and infertility. Still, this in no way provides proof that someone could be born the wrong sex. In fact, the symptoms of Klinefelter Syndrome can be minimized through medical treatments such as testosterone replacement therapy — proof that it is a disorder, not an issue of sexual identity.

GIVING UP THE FIGHT

I have heard several people who claim to be Christians, but have "come out of the closet" as homosexuals, say they finally decided to be true to themselves. In other words, being true to who they are meant they weren't going to fight their same-sex attractions anymore. But logically, a Christian is only true to who they are when they're doing their best to live according to the precepts of God.

For a man with same-sex attractions to say he is not going to fight it anymore is like a married heterosexual man with an attraction to other women saying he's not going to fight it anymore. His attraction to these women may be a continual temptation for him, but it is not acceptable according to the commandments of God to say he'll give in to his adulterous desires. Whether homosexual or heterosexual, giving up the battle against sin is not an option. As Paul wrote in 1 Timothy 6:11-12:

> But you, man of God, flee from all this, and pursue righteousness, godliness, faith, love, endurance and gentleness. Fight the good fight of the faith. Take hold of the

eternal life to which you were called when you made your good confession in the presence of many witnesses.

Make no mistake about it — homosexuality is a sin that gains a tremendous grip on its victims. But it's interesting that we as Christians don't condone or make provision for other behaviors that are sinful and/or harmful. We say that someone is "struggling" with an addiction to alcohol, gambling, tobacco, or pornography. So why would we condone, let alone celebrate, homosexual behavior? By the way, if someone says with transparency that they are "struggling" with a same-sex attraction, that is actually

not all bad. It means they recognize it as something that should be battled against, just like any other temptation that Satan would bring their way.

BEING A SWORD-FIGHTER

Remember, temptation is not sin. It is only when we dwell on it in our minds or act on it that temptation becomes sin. Jesus Himself was tempted by Satan in the desert in Matthew 4:1-11. Satan actually used Scripture in a twisted way, just as is done so many times today, to try and convince Jesus that a sinful response to the temptation would be acceptable. But the key for Jesus was that He *really knew* the Scriptures so Satan wasn't able to deceive Him. That is how we must deal with the "Did God really say...?" deception that is so commonly used to justify sexual sin today.

Just like Jesus, when we are talking about sex before marriage, adultery, homosexuality, etc. we need to learn the related Scriptures and trust in them as God's truth. As Paul wrote in Ephesians 6:17, we must equip ourselves with "the sword of the Spirit, which is the word of God." And we must reject the quasi-explanations that appear to justify sinful behavior.

THE DARKNESS OF ENLIGHTENMENT

It's interesting that for the six thousand or so years of man's existence, no legitimate theologian had ever questioned the sinfulness of homosexuality. Yet recently, a very few people have somehow received a revelation that *all* of those serious Bible scholars from *all* of those centuries were *all* wrong. It is simply unreasonable to believe in this recent "enlightenment" unless you want it to fit with an agenda.

You may have heard some of the modern arguments already. For instance, relating to the Old Testament, some gay advocates will point to passages such as Leviticus 20:13 which say those who participate in homosexual activity "must be put to death." They mock this as barbaric, saying it invalidates the credibility of the Scriptures on the subject of homosexuality and therefore should be ignored. But, just as many of the ceremonial and sacrificial laws are no longer binding under the New Covenant through Jesus, so too many of the Old Testament punishments are no longer binding. We can know what remains valid today because the required behaviors and responses are reiterated in the New Testament.

For example, in John 8 the teachers of the law and the Pharisees brought a woman to Jesus who had been caught in the act of adultery. They said she should be stoned, while reminding Jesus of the words of Leviticus 20:10 which called for adulterers to be put to death. In one of the more well-known passages of Scripture, Jesus told the assembled crowd in verse 7: "If any of you is without sin, let him be the first to throw a stone at her." One by one the crowd left because they all knew they were not guiltless. Jesus then told the woman to go and "leave your life of sin." So there you have it. Under the New Covenant, there is no stoning — just a requirement to sincerely repent and begin a new lifestyle of righteousness.

Other quasi-arguments favoring the acceptability of homosexuality relate to New Testament Scripture. The passage I shared earlier from Romans 1:26 seems pretty cut and dried when you read it without an agenda. This time I'll return to the New International Version: "Even their women exchanged natural relations for unnatural ones. In the same way the men also abandoned natural relations with women and were inflamed with lust for one another."

The argument from some gay advocates is that this passage is talking about *heterosexual* men and women engaging in *homosexual* activity. That, they say, is what is unnatural. Therefore, it is not addressing true homosexuals because it is natural for them to participate in homosexual activity.

But when you look again at the NASB version of this passage, which most pastors believe to be the most accurate word for word translation, it helps us realize this explanation is merely a hope-filled attempt to justify sinful behavior. In the NASB, "natural relations" is translated as "the natural function." As we discussed earlier the "natural function" is clearly reflected in the design of the male and female anatomy; they belong together, just like a nut and a bolt. Any other interpretation of this passage is simply not accurate.

There has also been an attempt to reinterpret 1 Corinthians 6:9 which, as we saw earlier, says that "homosexual offenders" are among those who will not "inherit the kingdom of heaven." The false teaching states that this is an incorrect interpretation of the original Greek words. I have seen complex explanations as to why this translation is wrong, relating to what the words actually meant at the time they were written, or what they meant when they were first translated in the King James Version as "the effeminate." Among other things, I have heard it said that these words were not specifically about sexuality, but had more to do with men who were either lazy or "soft," exhibiting certain female traits and behaviors.

Since the first printing of the King James Version some four hundred years ago, additional ancient biblical manuscripts have been discovered which have helped with clarification. That, coupled with increased understanding of the original languages of the Bible, has led to numerous modern translations. Hundreds of scholars have put in countless hours on the various new versions in an effort to assure accuracy. And no less than twelve of these versions translate 1 Corinthians 6:9 using the words *homosexuality*, *homosexual*, or *homosexuals.*

I heard somebody say one time that the more ingredients you find listed on the label of a package of food, the less pure and healthy the contents are. I believe the same applies here for those who advocate for the acceptance of homosexuality. Their explanation for why homosexual behavior is not condemned in 1 Corinthians 6:9 is so lengthy and convoluted that certainly the pure, healthy, spiritual meaning of the translation is being lost. So please, *please*, don't be fooled by any quasi-explanations. Take the pure, healthy contents of the Bible at face value and respond to them accordingly for eternity's sake.

One additional argument that is often used by gay advocates is the fact that Jesus never directly talked about homosexuality, at least as recorded in the Scriptures. They make the case that if homosexual activity was such a heinous sin, then certainly Jesus would have condemned it. But if that made gay behavior acceptable, then it would stand to reason that what is written in the rest of the Bible is fallible and unimportant. Because as we've seen, the issue is addressed many times in both the Old and New Testaments. Besides, even though Jesus didn't address homosexual behavior directly, He did reaffirm God's design for marriage and sexuality in Matthew 19:4-6:

> "Haven't you read...that at the beginning the Creator 'made them male and female,' and said, 'For this reason a man will leave his father and mother and be united to his wife, and the two will become one flesh'? So they are no longer two but one. Therefore what God has joined together, let man not separate."

Jesus leaves no room here for compromise or hedging. He begins and ends with the supposition that the only acceptable expression of sexuality is within the context of marriage between one man and one woman.

REDEFINING MARRIAGE

The overall feeling of the American people toward homosexuality has gone in just one generation from disdain, to tolerance, to acceptance, to endorsement. With this rapid advancement has come the highly successful call for total acknowledgment of same-sex relationships. Between the courts, state legislatures and Congress, so-called gay marriage has made the remarkable move toward becoming legal throughout the United States. And although the public had been soundly against allowing gay "marriage" just a few short years ago, the tide has been quickly turning.

Back in 1996, Congress overwhelmingly passed the Defense of Marriage Act with bipartisan support. It affirmed that the only marriages the federal government would recognize as legal were those between one man and one woman. Less than twenty years later in 2013, the Supreme Court found that law to be unconstitutional. Similar state-level DOMA laws throughout the country then began to fall. And by June 2015 the high court ruled in a 5-4 decision that same-sex couples have a constitutional right to marry, effectively legalizing gay unions across the nation. (It's interesting that, after more than two hundred years, God's design for marriage was suddenly found by five black-robed judges to be unconstitutional in the U.S.)

Why is the opportunity to marry so important to same-sex couples? There are certainly financial reasons, such as being able to legally obtain spousal benefits through a place of employment or for tax purposes. There are other advantages such as visiting privileges at hospitals. And there are those who truly want to express their love for one another by "taking the marital plunge."

Ironically, some also get "married" for a spiritual reason. Many of these couples say they are Christians, even though they are unapologetic about their homosexual relationships. They believe "marrying" their partner will somehow make their union acceptable in the eyes of God. (This again brings to mind the Old Testament patriarchs who chose to make wives out of their large number of sexual partners, no doubt convincing themselves that this sanctified their sinful behavior.)

This belief is supported by many people who call themselves Christians, including some clergy, who have been teaching that God approves of gay "marriage." I am deeply concerned that they, and those who believe what they say, are subjecting themselves to eternal danger. Jesus said in Matthew 7:21: "Not everyone who says to me, 'Lord, Lord,' will enter the kingdom of heaven, but only he who does the will of my Father who is in heaven."

I can only imagine the terror faced by these individuals one day when they realize they were wrong. They will have believed they did so much for the Lord. But Jesus goes on to say in verse 23 that none of this matters if we are not committed to living in obedience to God in our heart of hearts: "Then I will tell them plainly, 'I never knew you. Away from me, you evildoers.'"

It must be understood that God cannot be fooled. He knows the intent of our hearts, and our actions should flow out of hearts that are consecrated to Him. We cannot somehow work our way around God's clear commandments and expect to find favor in his eyes — for now or for eternity. Just as with the patriarchs, when we choose to make our own rules about what is sin or not we will eventually suffer great consequences. My prayer is that Jesus' warning will cause each person to turn from their disobedience so the consequence is merely earthly, not eternal.

THE CONSEQUENCE OF CONVICTION

The issue of same-sex marriage has actually become much bigger than simply a matter of gay rights. It is rapidly being used in our culture to draw a line in the sand as a way of punishing Christians who would stand up for biblical truth. We as believers are allowed to live according to our consciences, so far, except when it moves against the gay agenda. Civil rights laws all across the country are being amended to accommodate gay rights to the exclusion of religious rights.

Numerous examples abound, even in states where gay marriage is not yet legal. In Colorado, the Christian owner of a bake shop told a homosexual couple that based on his religious convictions he could not create a cake for their gay wedding. He did offer to sell them any other baked goods in his store, indicating this was not a case of discrimination, just conviction. But that wasn't good enough. The couple filed a complaint with the state, and as a result, the owner was ordered to undergo sensitivity training, and was required to ensure that his staff became "rehabilitated" in their thinking regarding the accommodation of gay weddings.

In Minnesota, the Christian owner of a lodge that frequently hosted wedding receptions politely turned down a request to host a reception following a gay ceremony as a matter of his religious convictions. Rather than find an alternative location, the homosexual couple filed a complaint against the lodge. Under the threat of sanctions by the state, the owner agreed to not only host the reception, but to pay for it as well.

This has clearly become more than a gay rights issue. These are just two examples of many across the nation where Christians are being forced by the government to act in violation of their religious beliefs. And such "civil rights" laws have begun to impact more than just Christian-owned businesses. They have now been extended in certain cases to cover churches and ministers — something advocates of these laws assured us would never happen.

For example, in October 2014 five pastors in Houston, Texas were subpoenaed by the city and their mayor, who is an admitted lesbian, to turn over their sermons, speeches, and other communications relating to their opposition to a new civil rights ordinance. Among other things, the law would have allowed men who self-identify as women to use women's restrooms and vice versa. The pastors were told that if they refused to cooperate they could face fines or jail time. This obvious violation of freedom of religion and freedom of speech was headed to the courts at the time of this writing.

Then, less than a week later, the husband and wife owners of a wedding chapel in Coeur d'Alene, Idaho were told that they too could face possible fines or jail time for refusing to perform a same-sex wedding ceremony. The owners were ordained Christian ministers who had performed wedding ceremonies at the chapel since 1989. The city said their refusal was a violation of its non-discrimination ordinance. It's a chilling reality that so-called "gay rights" are now trumping religious and free speech rights in the United States, despite the fact that the latter are suppose to be guaranteed in the First Amendment of the Constitution.

These are vivid examples of what I stated earlier — the issue of gay rights is rapidly being used in our culture to draw a line in the sand, punishing Christians who would stand up for biblical truth. If followers of Jesus can be forced to go against their convictions on one issue, who's to say they won't be required to forsake their beliefs on other critical issues of spiritual importance in the future?

A GREATER PURPOSE IN THE DESIGN

But pastors, and all Christians, are called to stand up for God's truth no matter what the consequences. And His design for marriage can literally be found from Genesis to Revelation in the Bible. I've already shared the Scripture passage where God laid the foundation for marriage right at the beginning in Genesis 2:22-24.

In the fifth of the Ten Commandments found in Exodus 20:12 and again in Deuteronomy 5:16, God's design for marriage and families is in no way ambiguous: "Honor your father and your mother, as the Lord your God has commanded you..."

This is reiterated in the New Testament in Ephesians 6:1-2. Also in Ephesians, we see that there is a greater purpose in God's design for marriage in 5:22-33. In select portions of this passage we see that marriage is meant to reflect the relationship between Jesus and the Church...

> Wives, submit to your husbands as to the Lord. For the husband is the head of the wife as Christ is the head of the church, his body, of which he is the Savior...Husbands love your wives, just as Christ loved the church and gave himself up for her...This is a profound mystery — but I am talking about Christ and the church.

And it's worth noting that the Genesis 2:24 design for marriage, one man and one woman becoming one flesh, is quoted yet again in these verses in Ephesians. The husband in a marriage represents Christ, and the wife represents we who make up the Church.

PROPER SUBMISSION IS A PROFITABLE COMMISSION

Before we move on, I want to take a moment to address an often misunderstood and abused aspect of biblical marriage which is mentioned in this passage from Ephesians 5. It's a tragedy that submission in marriage has often been looked at incorrectly as permission for the husband to be domineering and overbearing with his wife. Because of this, women today have routinely come to despise the word "submit." But under the biblical design, submission can be more properly understood in terms of "chain of command."

As an example, marriage can be loosely compared to the relationship between a wise president and his vice-president. When the president has an important decision to make, he seeks the valuable input of the vice-president. He then makes his decision based on what he thinks is best for their good and the good of the country. Because he has been given the most authority, the president ultimately is held accountable for his decision by the citizens who put him in power.

Similarly, when an important decision has to be made in a healthy marriage, the wise husband seeks the valuable input of his wife. He then makes the decision based on what he thinks is best for their marriage and family. Because he has been given the most authority, the husband is ultimately held accountable for his decision by God, the One who put him in that position.

In another example, anyone who has been in the military understands the importance of chain of command. When each soldier recognizes the established level of authority, there is order when they face a battle and therefore a greater likelihood of success. And a good leader will seek out valuable reconnaissance from those under his command to help him in making wise decisions for their collective victory. If anyone tries to succeed by doing their own thing, there is likely chaos and failure.

In the same way, when God's chain of command is honored in the home and the husband's authority is properly understood, the chances for success when facing life's challenges are much greater. And the wise husband will seek out his wife's input so they can win the "battles" together. But if they try to succeed by doing their own thing, they are much more likely to fail.

So submission — biblically speaking — doesn't lead to extra privilege for the husband, but rather, extra responsibility. And it's meant for the good of the family, not to meet his selfish desires. Those who would say wives need to be quietly subjected to tyrannical husbands are simply sharing a false teaching. Any doubt about this is erased in 1 Peter 3:7:

> Husbands, in the same way be considerate as you live with your wives, and treat them with respect as the weaker partner and as heirs with you of the gracious gift of life, so that nothing will hinder your prayers.

Husbands need to take special note of this. If we do not treat our wives considerately and with respect, it literally hinders our prayers. That is how important this issue is to God!

THE BEST "CHURCH" WEDDING EVER

As we continue looking at marriage in the New Testament, Paul shares with young pastors Timothy and Titus what the qualifications for church leaders should be. Among his instructions in 1 Timothy 3:2 and Titus 1:6 is that leaders of the church must be "the husband of but one wife." This leaves absolutely no doubt that God's design for marriage, especially among those committed to His service, is one man and one woman.

And in Revelation 19:7, Jesus — the bridegroom — returns for the wedding with His bride — the Church — at the Glorious Appearing: "Let us rejoice and be glad and give him glory! For the wedding of the Lamb has come, and his bride has made herself ready." No room is given in this passage for a marriage between two brides, or two grooms, or more than one of either. So literally, God's design for marriage — one man and one woman for life — can be found in the Bible from Genesis to Revelation.

END TIMES THREATS TO MARRIAGE

Biblical marriage is under an intense, supernatural attack in these last days. It's ironic that while large numbers of heterosexual couples have been choosing to reject marriage as an outdated, unnecessary practice, homosexual couples have been battling hard for the right to get married legally. To me, this indicates an obvious spiritual battle. Whatever the sexual orientation, there appears to be an orchestrated rebellion against God's design for marriage and sexuality. Not only does this threaten to tear down individual lives and society, but Satan knows that making marriage "optional" or redefining it into what man wants it to be ultimately skews the proper understanding of Christ's relationship with His Church.

One final thought on marriage. What should a Christian do if they are invited to attend a so-called gay wedding? I hadn't planned to address this issue, but the question came up more than once while I was writing this book so I decided it was a topic worthy of discussion. Some had said they didn't know what they would do if asked. Others said they would accept such an invitation as a way of showing the love of Christ to the gay couple. But I have come to the conclusion this would clearly be the wrong course of action.

First of all, if you are invited to a "gay wedding" it is likely the couple already understands you care about them as individuals. Otherwise you wouldn't have been invited in the first place. But even if the invitation was obligatory, such as in the case of close relatives, I believe participation would still send the wrong message when considering the broader picture.

Attending a "gay wedding" would in effect be an endorsement of something that is an affront to God. Why would a Christian want to celebrate something that at its very core dishonors the Lord? I had asked that question to a Christian who said he would attend the "wedding" of a same-sex couple if invited. Interestingly, he compared that to participating in the wedding of a heterosexual couple that had become pregnant before their marriage. He said it was basically the same thing because both couples would have been guilty of sexual sin.

I strongly disagreed. I told him that the heterosexual couple was doing their best to *honor* God from that time forward by getting married. Like the woman caught in adultery in John 8, they were following Jesus' command to "leave your life of sin." In a complete contrast, gay couples who get "married" are publicly displaying their intent to *dishonor* God with their sexuality for the rest of their lives.

If I were asked to attend a so-called gay wedding, I would do my very best to let the couple know I love them with the love of Christ but I could not in good conscience attend the ceremony based on my commitment to God. The best way we can show anyone who is living a sinful lifestyle that we love them is by letting them know we care more about their eternal destination than their temporal happiness. And then I would encourage them with all sincerity to reconsider the choice they are making.

CONCLUDING THOUGHT

To followers of Jesus, homosexuality has often been a focus of criticism because so few have actually struggled with same-sex attractions. A far greater number have been tempted to have sex before marriage, or during marriage with someone who is not their spouse. As we saw in the previous chapter, these are *all* sinful acts in the eyes of God so none of us has the privilege of being self-righteous.

Does God love those who practice homosexuality? Absolutely. But can they continue in their behavior unrepentantly? Of course not. None of us is given permission to remain in our sin. We are expected to do all we can to forsake sinful lifestyles to the glory of God. To overcome the strong grip of sexual temptations, we need to invite the Holy Spirit to take control of our lives by making it a disciplined practice of studying our Bibles and praying every day. And there is no shame in seeking help. Trusted Bible-believing pastors or Christian counselors can provide needed support when the battle seems too much to fight alone. Calling on a close friend to be an accountability partner has also been shown to have a great track record of success.

I encourage you to remember, that when you do fall, never give up and never quit trying. It may take some time, but as you commit to honoring God with your sexuality, I truly believe He will bless you with ultimate victory!

9–THE BROAD ROAD: ISLAM

*Simply put, in order to have eternal life you have to believe
in Jesus as the Son of God, that He died on a cross for
your sins, rose again, and then confess him as your Lord.
Muslims believe none of this.*

There once was a man who went to an airport with the intention of flying to a tropical paradise. The only problem was he had not purchased a ticket for the flight in advance. There was only one airline that flew to this particular destination, so he attempted to buy a ticket on the spot. But the man didn't carefully read the brochure which said the airline required each passenger to have an advanced purchase agreement before they could be admitted onto the flight. So he was turned away by the ticketing agent.

The man also failed to notice the brochure clearly stated that this airline provided the only way to the paradise. So he decided he would just go to another airline and buy a ticket from them. After all, he had seen many advertisements for these other airlines talking up their many wonderful attributes. These convincing ads made the man believe he could go anywhere he wanted on any one of these airlines. But while each offered many nice perks, like in-flight meals and movies, none of them could take him to his desired destination. The man could enjoy the journey, but when it came right down to it, he would never reach the paradise he was hoping for.

It's probably obvious that this is not a true story, but rather, an analogy to illustrate a very important point. In recent years, the belief that there are many ways to reach an eternal home with God has been growing in popularity. Similar to this man, there are many who want to reach paradise (heaven) but have not purchased a ticket in advance as stated in the brochure (accepted Jesus as Savior and Lord before their death as recorded in the Scriptures). So in the end, they are turned away.

Despite what the Bible clearly states, there are many today who try to find another way to paradise. The false religions may sound enticing, and many offer attractive sounding "perks." But no matter how wonderful they appear to be, and no matter how strongly a person may believe in them, these false religions will never be able to take a person to their desired destination. Only true Christianity ends up in paradise.

NOT A HOLY MANIPULATION

According to many, the most important thing is to be sincere in your belief, and try to live a good life along the way. Of course, postmodernism would say that what constitutes a "good life" is, to a certain extent, based on your own beliefs. You shouldn't hurt other people, but after that, living a good life is largely up to your own interpretation.

As with so many other dangerous beliefs, the thought pervading the culture that there are many ways to heaven is invading the Kingdom of God at the same time. This is despite the fact that the Bible contains many, *many* passages declaring that only through Jesus can we spend our eternity with God.

Matthew 7:13-14 is the foundational passage for the next four chapters of this book. Jesus said:

Enter through the narrow gate. For wide is the gate and broad is the road that leads to destruction, and many enter through it. But small is the gate and narrow the road that leads to life, and only a few find it.

Jesus said these prophetic words as part of His famed Sermon on the Mount where a large crowd from across the region had gathered to hear Him speak. Jesus was talking about the reality that most people will ultimately choose to reject Him and spend their eternity separated from God. By saying this, was Jesus trying to scare them into following Him — a kind of holy manipulation? Of course not. Jesus never sinned, so we know He would not tell a lie as a way of deceiving people into accepting salvation. No, Jesus said this because it is the truth — a truth that we have to come to grips with whether we like it or not.

Many people across the centuries *haven't* liked this truth, so they've come up with their own versions of reality. These come in the form of false teachings, false religions, and cults. In doing so, they have actually done their part to fulfill this prophecy, leading large masses to the "broad road" that leads to eternal destruction. I'm going to address several of the most prominent of these beliefs, not as a way of bashing them or their followers, but simply to point out the differences between them and what the Bible says. Because any belief that varies from the absolute truth of Scripture is by definition false.

ANSWERS IN HISTORY

The first broad road I've chosen to discuss is Islam because of the fact that, apart from Christianity, it is the largest and most influential spiritual belief in the world today. Literally every day the actions of Muslims, the followers of Islam, are in the news. Most of it is very bad, including atrocities such as the beheadings of those who reject Islam; suicide bombings which target innocent men, women and children; and abductions of young women who are forced to become "wives" (essentially sex slaves) of their captors. We are routinely told by politicians, the media, and "moderate" Muslims that these things do not represent true Islam. So what should we believe?

To gain understanding, it is helpful to look at the origins of the religion. The founder of Islam is Mohammed, who was born in 570 AD in the land that is now Saudi Arabia. He learned much about Christianity and Judaism while growing up. This is an important fact because the Qur'an contains many surahs, or chapters, that share common people and themes with the Bible. These apparent similarities have helped boost the false perception that Christians and Muslims worship the same God.

In 610 AD, while meditating in a cave near Mecca, Mohammed is said to have received "revelations" from God, delivered through the angel Gabriel. (The mention of Gabriel is one of the perceived similarities to the Bible.) It has been said that Mohammed could not read or write so he shared his revelations with others who would copy them down. These became the initial writings of the Qur'an, Islam's main "holy book." Subsequent "revelations" would continue to be added to the Qur'an throughout Mohammed's life.

While in Mecca, the surahs were quite genteel, compassionate, and inclusive. This was during a time when the fledgling religion was weak and struggling for acceptance. Some examples:

- Referencing the opponents of Islam, surah 73:10 says:
  "Be patient with what they say, and part from them courteously."

- Surah 2:256 tells Muslims not to impose Islam by force:
  "There is no compulsion in religion."

- Muslims are instructed to peacefully advocate for Islam when speaking with Jews and Christians in surah 29:46:
  "Argue with the people of the Book, other than evil doers, only by means of what is better! And say, we believe in what has been sent down to us and sent down to you. Our God is the same as your God, and we are surrendered to him."

In 622 AD Mohammed faced danger because of his teachings so he and his small group of followers fled to Medina. There, Islam began to grow in numbers and in subsequent strength. When this happened, Mohammed changed and so did his "revelations." He became a fierce warrior and began to spread his religion by the sword. During this time, the surahs took on a very different tone:

- Rather than patience with the opponents of Islam as we saw in the Meccan surahs, Muslims are told to murder their opposition in surah 2:191: "Kill them wherever you find them, and drive them out from wherever they drove you out..."

- Also in surah 2:191, Islam is no longer to be spread simply by peaceful means: "Fight (kill) them until there is no persecution and the religion is God's."

- Muslims are instructed in surah 9:29 that Jews and Christians are no longer to be tolerated: "Fight those who do not believe in God and the last day...and fight the people of the Book, who do not accept the religion of truth (Islam) until they pay tribute by hand, being inferior."

These teachings were what drove the rapid spread of Islam throughout most of Arabia by the time of Mohammed's death in 632 AD. His followers continued to advance the religion through largely violent means. Non-Muslims were forced to either convert, live in poverty, or be put to death. Unless their spiritual conviction was strong, whether for Christianity or something else, people would likely convert just to avoid a harsh life of persecution. Within one hundred years after Mohammed died, Muslims had conquered what we know today as the Middle East (including Israel), North Africa, and Spain.

ABROGATION–A CAUSE FOR CONFUSION

By looking at the contradiction between the Meccan and Medinian surahs, it is easy to see why there is such confusion as to who the real Muslims are; the peace-loving "moderates" who condemn violent jihad (holy war), or the so-called radicals who are committing the atrocities I mentioned earlier. Your belief on this depends on your understanding of the Qur'an, and to a certain extent, where you live.

Similar to the time of Mohammed, in countries like the United States where Islam is not dominant you will find, for the most part, peaceful Muslims who live by the Meccan surahs. These are also the surahs that are regularly quoted by those who try to cast Islam in a positive light. Unfortunately, this is either a naive or deceptive practice.

Those who have a comprehensive understanding of the Qur'an — like those who speak Arabic, the original language in which it was written – know there is a concept in Islamic doctrine called abrogation. According to former Muslim Abdullah Al Araby, who founded the website www.islamreview.com, this doctrine is based on two passages in the Qur'an. Surah 2:106 says, "None of our revelations do we abrogate or cause to be forgotten, but we substitute something better or similar. Knowest thou not that Allah hath power over all things?" And surah 16:101 states, "When we substitute one revelation for another, and Allah knows best what he reveals (in stages), they say, 'Thou art but a forger': but most of them understand not."

Basically abrogation means that when one surah in the Qur'an contradicts another surah, then the newer passage is considered better and replaces the previous passage. Therefore the harsher, more violent Medinian surahs render the related, more peaceful Meccan surahs that were written earlier as null and void. There are many examples of this. In fact, of the 114 surahs in the Qur'an, 71 have been affected by the doctrine of abrogation.

So those who are classified as "radical" Muslims, most of who come from Arabic speaking countries in the Middle East, are the ones who are more tuned in to the actual teachings of the Qur'an. We already looked at some of the Medinian surahs that endorse violent jihad as a way of advancing Islam. And I believe it is actually incorrect to classify those who practice their religion in this way as "extremists."

According to a Pew Research study released in August 2014, a worldwide average of 72 percent of Muslims is opposed to violence in the name of Islam; some may be among your good friends and neighbors. While that's a strong majority, it still means 28 percent of Muslims are OK with the thought of physical harm against those who don't adhere to Islam. With an estimated 1.3 billion Muslims in the world as of this writing, that means more than 360 million of them condone violence as a way of advancing the cause of Islam. If they were a country, their population would exceed that of the United States! This is no extreme fringe we're talking about here.

CONFUSION IN HISTORY

There are those who get tripped up by the fact that both the Old Testament of the Bible and portions of the Qur'an contain discussions about the opponents of God getting slaughtered at the hands of believers. This appears to make Christianity no better than Islam when it comes to the treatment of those who disagree with their faith. But there is a very important and undeniable difference.

The Old Testament is a historical record of the events that took place prior to the birth of Jesus. It does not contain any doctrine instructing New Covenant, modern day believers to kill those who are opposed to God. On the contrary, Jesus told his followers to love and pray for their enemies (Matthew 5:44). In total contrast, as we saw in the Medinian surahs (which abrogated the more peaceful Meccan surahs) there is plenty of instruction for modern day Muslims to fight, kill, and otherwise oppress those who will not submit to Islam.

I'd like to set the record straight on another historical misunderstanding that has been used to incite Muslims in their hatred toward Christianity — military actions beginning near the turn of the twelfth century that have come to be known as the Crusades. We have been led to believe the Crusades were fiendish actions by greedy Christians against peaceful Muslims. While I am leaving out a huge amount of detail, suffice it to say there were several Crusades, or military endeavors, that were endorsed by the Catholic popes who were very powerful at that time.

Shortly after its founding in the seventh century, Islam had overtaken by the sword many lands once dominated by Christianity and life in these areas became very harsh for faithful believers. They appealed to the popes over the course of many years for deliverance from their bondage. This resulted in the first Crusade in 1095. In truth, this military action was intended to end the tyranny against these Christians. So to say the Crusades were unprovoked attacks against innocent Muslims is simply not true.

Any belief that the popes or crusaders were greedy plunderers is also patently false. The Christians who were recruited to take part in the Crusades did not in any way reap a financial windfall. In fact, they generally believed they would not come out alive — dying as martyrs doing the will of God. Most plunder taken from their conquered Muslim enemies was used to finance their military efforts, a common practice among armies in that era. In truth, the popes regularly struggled in their attempts to properly fund the Crusades.

In keeping with the commonly believed narrative, there were occasional atrocities committed by some of the crusaders, but it was not an endorsed practice. When we look at the modern U.S. military campaigns, such as those in Vietnam or the Middle East, we have heard of occasional acts of brutality committed by a very small number of our own troops. But we wouldn't want the United States to be defined by the disgraceful actions of an undisciplined few. The same can be said for the vast number of Christians who wouldn't want their faith defined by the shameful actions of a few rogue crusaders, supposedly in the name of Christ.

It's interesting to note that the Crusades were a largely forgotten aspect of history among Muslims for many centuries. The rhetoric that the Crusades were all about innocent Muslims being victimized by cruel Christians actually was spread beginning in the early twentieth century as a propaganda tool to mobilize

Islam against the West. Sadly, this idea has been almost universally accepted as truth and is still being used to recruit Islamic militants to this day.

DISCOURAGING DOUBLE-STANDARDS

The spirit-realm battle between Christianity and Islam can be seen in double-standards that are running amok today. Unless you think in terms of spiritual warfare, it makes no sense that following 9/11 — when professed Muslims killed thousands of innocent people — the followers of Islam actually grew in number. Political leaders were among those who went out of their way to say this did not represent real Islam, and overall, the religion was actually elevated in respect and reputation.

Can you imagine if self-professed Christians committed such atrocities? We would all be brushed with a broad stroke of condemnation and it would take years to live it down, if ever. The Klu Klux Klan has historically *claimed* to be Christian, saying their racist hatred and violence that peaked in the early twentieth century has been endorsed by their biblical beliefs. This is absurd, but many have bought the lie and we as true believers are still considered by many as accomplices in those evil deeds.

Another glaring double-standard can be found in our public schools. Prayer in school was declared unconstitutional by the U.S. Supreme Court in the 1960's and has been banned ever since. But recently, many schools have begun providing special accommodations for Muslim students to pray during school hours. One school district that is leading the way is in Dearborn, Michigan, a suburb of Detroit, which has the largest Islamic population in the United States. Under a settlement negotiated in 2013 with the Muslim advocacy organization Council on American-Islamic Relations, or CAIR, the Dearborn school board voted to allow for "student-led" prayers in the district's schools.

By contrast, in September 2014 a high school in Colorado Springs, Colorado banned a group of Christian students from praying, singing spiritual songs, and conducting Bible studies during their free time. As a designated part of the school day, each student could use the time as desired — academically, recreationally, or otherwise. For three years the group of Christian students had been meeting together in an unoccupied choir room to pray and otherwise grow in their faith. The school district eventually decided this was a violation of the so-called separation of church and state; this despite the fact that these spiritual activities were "student-led."

Finally, I want to discuss the reaction to an attempt by a Florida pastor to burn Qur'ans in 2013 on the anniversary of the 9/11 attacks. Riots broke out in a number of places throughout the Muslim world, with buildings being torched and many people killed. I can remember much of the media commentary from that time being sympathetic of the Muslims who were so "deeply offended" at the actions of this pastor. Meanwhile, the pastor was vilified as if no worse evil had ever been committed. One newspaper writer even called him a "whack-job pastor." So much for unbiased, balanced reporting.

Make no mistake about it, I believe that pastor's actions lacked any sense of wisdom whatsoever and were in no way productive or Christ-like. However, it is nothing short of bizarre to make him out to be more of a villain than the people halfway around the world that were burning up buildings and murdering innocent people as a result of being "offended."

What happens if somebody burns Bibles? It wouldn't even make the news. Even if it did, there would be no violence or rioting. True Christians would allow God to deal with the situation; it's not our fight. We are instructed to respond with the love of Christ to those who have perpetrated an offense against us (Matthew 5:44). This is a concept that is difficult for a Muslim, or any other non-Christian, to understand.

A QUESTION OF PATERNITY

The varied responses to the burning of our respective "holy books" gives me an opportunity to transition to my main purpose for writing these "broad road" chapters — to provide understanding that Christianity is different from all other spiritual beliefs and is the one and only path to God. While Islam is often compared to Christianity and is considered just another route to the same destination, the contrasts between the two are stark. You've likely heard about marriages that were dissolved because of "irreconcilable differences." That is exactly what separates the beliefs of Islam and Christianity. Although these differences are many, I will only highlight two of the most crucial.

First, consider what Muslims believe about Jesus. They say he was a great prophet, but just one of many. And although the Qur'an says Jesus was born of a virgin named Mary, Muslims do not believe he was the son of God. The Bible on the other hand tells us a different story. In John 3:16-18 we read:

> For God so loved the world that he gave *his one and only Son*, that whoever believes in him shall not perish but have eternal life. For God did not send *his Son* into the world to condemn the world, but to save the world through him. Whoever believes in him is not condemned, but whoever does not believe stands condemned already because he has not believed in the name of *God's one and only Son*. (Emphasis added)

Muslims also do not believe that Jesus died on a cross or rose to life again. Surah 4:157-158 describes how the Jews tried to crucify Jesus but He didn't die because Allah rescued Him and took Him to heaven. However, the Bible says in Romans 5:8:

> But God demonstrates his own love for us in this: While we were still sinners, *Christ died for us*. (Emphasis added)

And in 1 Corinthians 15:3-6 we read:

> For what I received I passed on to you as of first importance: that *Christ died for our sins* according to the Scriptures, that he was buried, that he was raised on the third day according to the Scriptures, and that he appeared

to Peter, and then to the Twelve. After that, he appeared to more than five hundred of the brothers at the same time... (Emphasis added)

As you can see at the end of this passage the author, Paul, makes sure to emphasize that Jesus was seen by a multitude of witnesses after His crucifixion and burial, proving that He truly rose from the dead.

THE CERTAINTY OF SALVATION

This leads to a second crucial, irreconcilable difference between Islam and Christianity — salvation. The Qur'an teaches that there are two angels assigned to every person to record their good and bad deeds. If their goods deeds outweigh their bad, then Allah *may* allow them into heaven; it is still up to his discretion.

The only sure way to heaven is if a Muslim "martyrs" him or herself for the cause of Islam. That is why so many are willing to blow themselves up, or fly airplanes into buildings, etc. to kill "infidels" (non-Muslims). They believe they will be instantly trans-ported into heaven where, among other things, the men will have dozens of virgins waiting to fulfill their desires. You can see why young men are regularly the victims of this doctrine. Someone like an awkward, unattractive, perhaps acne-laden teenage boy would be especially vulnerable, believing his dreams will come true with adoring women waiting to overwhelm him with their attention and affection.

By the way, the term "martyr" in this situation is actually not accurate and is rather offensive. A martyr is someone who is killed by others because of their faith, like so many Christians who have steadfastly remained faithful to God no matter the cost. Someone who kills as many people as he can while taking his own life is in reality committing mass murder-suicide.

While salvation for the Muslim is filled with uncertainty, the Christian can be sure of his eternal destiny. In Romans 10:9-10 Paul wrote:

That if you confess with your mouth, 'Jesus is Lord,' and believe in your heart that God raised him from the dead, *you will be saved.* For it is with your heart that you believe and are justified, and it is with your mouth that you confess and are saved. (Emphasis added)

Simply put, in order to have eternal life you have to believe in Jesus as the Son of God, that He died on a cross for your sins, rose again, and then confess him as your Lord. Muslims believe none of this and therefore have not received salvation. This is not my standard; this is what the Bible says. With this in mind, Christians need to compassionately share the love of Jesus with Muslims, understanding that they have been imprisoned by a satanic deception. Unless they hear and accept the truth of the Gospel, they will end up in the eternal torment of hell.

MUSLIMS IN MAJORITY

Before we move on to the next broad road topic, I want to share a warning. We cannot be naive to the intent of Islam. The goal of devout Muslims is to one day conquer the world for Allah. They will not be forever content in countries like the United States to co-exist with people of other faiths. Muslim leaders have a multi-faceted plan for gaining majority status in countries where they are currently in the minority. This includes growing large families and pushing the limits of a country's immigration laws. In fact, a Pew Research study from August 2011 found that nearly two out of three adult Muslims living in the United States today were born in another country.

When their numbers make it possible, Muslim leaders routinely push for the implementation of Shariah Law. Islam is more than just a religion; it is a comprehensive way of life. Through the Qur'an and other religious writings such as the Hadith, Mohammed, his followers, and generations of Muslim theologians have prescribed numerous regulations governing every aspect of social, political, economic, and religious life. These regulations make up Shariah Law. This is why the requests by Muslims for special accommodations can't always be viewed as issues of religious freedom.

For example, under Shariah Law a man can be married to four women at the same time (surah 4:3), and can beat a wife who is disobedient to him (surah 4:34). If he gets charged with such a crime, the day may come in the United States that the man could ask the court for a religious exemption because these actions are legal under Islamic Shariah Law. It seems obvious that such abuses should in no way be viewed as spiritual issues, and currently they remain illegal in the U.S. But where Shariah Law is instituted, it trumps any existing national, state or local laws. So if the population trends continue, and there is no prudent vigilance to the nationalistic goals of Islam, it is possible that such crimes could one day become legal here.

If you doubt that, keep in mind that Islam is the fastest growing religion in the U.S. As of this writing, there are more than two thousand mosques, Islamic schools, and Islamic centers across the nation; more than 62 percent of these have been built since 1980. When Islam reaches about 5 percent of a nation's population, they begin to exert political and social pressures. Although the U.S. Muslim population is currently estimated at only about 2 percent, they are already asserting themselves here because of our "tolerant" religious attitudes.

As an example, in the previously mentioned Dearborn, Michigan, Christian Post contributor Gene Koprowski wrote in a June 2013 article that Christians "are second-class citizens, as if they are residents of an Islamic Republic, where they are considered infidels, without full civil rights. Local police departments refuse to allow Christians to distribute Bible-based literature for fear of infuriating Muslims, but let local Muslim preachers use the city's own loudspeaker system to announce daily calls to prayer."

What else could be expected if Shariah becomes the law of the land? We as Christians would no longer have the right to freely practice our faith. As non-Muslims who refuse to embrace Islam we would be ineligible for the best jobs, taxed into poverty, imprisoned, or even face death. And any Muslim who decided he wanted to leave Islam, such as those who are repulsed by the thought of violent jihad, would be subject to death (surah 9:12-14).

This could include children who are slain by their own parents, a practice known peculiarly in the Muslim world as "honor killings" (based on surah 18:80-81). Such an extreme action is not universally accepted among Muslims. But it still breaks my heart when I see cute little girls wearing hijabs, the female Muslim head-covering, knowing any road to their salvation would be paved with heartache. At the very least, they would be excommunicated from their families if they left Islam. And as I just mentioned, in extreme cases, their very lives could be in danger.

For those who doubt what I'm saying, all you have to do is look at regions of the world that are already dominated by Islam. Overall, these Muslim-majority countries are human rights train wrecks. The most basic rights that we in the United States take for granted —freedom of religion and freedom of speech among them — are a rarity for non-Muslims in these countries. And even those who *are* Muslims, but are women or so-called moderates, often find themselves treated as second-class citizens.

CONCLUDING THOUGHT

I've said it before, but it bears repeating. The purpose of doing a comparative analysis between other religions and Christianity is not to "bash" them. I'm simply trying to point out that there is no way to reconcile these beliefs with the truth of Scripture. I understand the desire to be tolerant and accepting of other peoples' spiritual convictions. It seems to be the most loving thing we can do — believe me, I get that. But what we want, and what is truth, are often quite different.

Actually, the most loving, compassionate thing we can do is share the truth of Jesus Christ with anyone caught up in a false belief system, understanding that they are being imprisoned by a satanic deception. Our hearts need to break at the thought that these people will end up in the eternal torment of hell unless they hear and accept the reality of the Gospel.

10–THE BROAD ROAD: EASTERN RELIGION & THE NEW AGE

New Age Spirituality is being used as a highly-successful tool of Satan. A broad-reaching mindset is being created across the earth in which people will have no trouble accepting a one-world government or religion. NAS would lead you to believe that all roads lead to God.

Perhaps you have enjoyed the excitement of a TV show or movie in which an innocent victim is befriended by a seemingly harmless, even friendly individual. Because they have developed trust in this person, the victim takes no precautions to guard themselves. Unbeknownst to the victim, the heretofore trusted individual has been lurking outside of the residence on a regular basis waiting for an opportunity to do them harm. Then one dark, quiet night the victim, in an unjustified feeling of security, fails to lock the door to their residence.

As the dramatic music ramps up the door slowly begins to open with an eerie creak. You're on the edge of your seat when this dangerous individual enters the residence because of the complete vulnerability of the victim. Without even realizing it, they are totally at the mercy of the merciless. Unless someone intervenes, the victim will soon succumb to painful consequences due to their lack of discernment to the danger.

This is very much the type of scenario I see in relation to our next broad road topic. Eastern religions, such as Hinduism and the closely related Buddhism, are having a major impact on the world today. Their influence among Western cultures has grown dramatically in recent years largely because of their acceptance as part of the New Age Movement — or as it is more commonly known today, New Age Spirituality, or even just New Spirituality. These beliefs may seem harmless. But in the end, nothing could be further from the truth. They are a merciless deception from Satan, and many who have naively believed the friendly facade have suffered painful consequences for their lack of discernment to the danger.

HINDUISM AND THE REINCARNATION RESOLVE

There are about 790 million Hindus worldwide, comprising about 13 percent of the world's population. India is the center of Hinduism, but one million Hindus live in the United States, mostly in New York, Los Angeles, and San Francisco.

Although Hinduism is polytheistic with millions of gods, the main god is Brahma, known as the Impersonal Absolute or the Ultimate Reality. The utmost goal of Hinduism is to break free from the "individual soul" and unite with the "universal soul." This comes from the Hindu belief in pantheism, that all is God and God is all. Once this happens, the "mature" Hindu becomes one with the Ultimate Reality. This process is accomplished through the death/birth cycle of reincarnation and karma.

Reincarnation is the belief that after you die, you will be born again into a new life. That life will either be better or worse, depending on the karma you produced in the previous life. Karma has to do with good works and bad works. The more "good karma" you produce, the more likely the next life will be better on the way to uniting with the universal soul.

It should be noted that most Hindus also believe in transmigration. While reincarnation would dictate that humans return in the next life as another human, transmigration allows for those with very bad karma to return in other life forms such as bugs or animals.

Among the methods used by Hindus to reach a mystical union with the universal soul are meditation and yoga. These related techniques were developed by a guru named Pantanjali about two thousand years ago, and he and other guru masters would teach them as a way of achieving supreme concentration on the Ultimate Reality. (We'll discuss this in more detail in a moment.)

BUDDHISM AND THE ENLIGHTENMENT EFFORT

Buddhism is a closely related, but distinctly different, cousin of Hinduism. While Hinduism is polytheistic with millions of gods, Buddhism is actually atheistic with no god; all spirituality is achieved through self-discovery and awareness. In essence, the goal of a Buddhist is to achieve a godlike "enlightenment."

There are more than 350 million Buddhists worldwide, most of whom reside in China, Japan, Korea and Southeast Asia. The Buddhist population in the United States is approximately 500 thousand, and is the main religion in Hawaii.

Buddhists believe in reincarnation, but in a different way than the Hindu. While Hindus believe the various lives provide an opportunity to move closer to oneness with their cosmic god (the Ultimate Reality), Buddhists believe the evils of greed, hatred, and ignorance can be overcome through reincarnation. Eventually, the realization of ultimate truth and understanding is achieved — an enlightenment known as nirvana. There is an eight-step process to nirvana known as the Noble Eightfold Path. I won't expound on this, other than to say it is a works-based process that encourages right living with many of the same godly virtues found in the Bible.

Meditation is the central process by which Buddhists pursue nirvana. It is a practice, similar to Hinduism, in which a mantra such as "Om" is repeated over and over as a way of achieving mental calmness. Of course, meditation for Buddhists is not prayer since Buddhism has no god. It is rather an attempt to awaken a source of spiritual power from within themselves.

Many people mistakenly believe that Buddha is the god of Buddhism. But in reality, that was a designation given to the religion's founder, Siddhartha, in the sixth century BC. His followers began calling him "the Buddha," a Sanskrit word which means "the Enlightened One." Siddhartha was only the first Buddha; as people supposedly reach the goal of enlightened status, or nirvana, they too become Buddhas.

THE NEW AGE: NOTHING AND EVERYTHING AT THE SAME TIME

The United States has become fertile ground in recent years for the advance of Eastern religions, but as I mentioned earlier, under the much more palatable label of New Age Spirituality (NAS). This is a belief system that is hard to pin down. It has no formal structure or statement of beliefs; it actually consists of an inclusive mix of many existing spiritual beliefs.

In their book *World Religions and Cults 101*, Bruce Bickel and Stan Jantz say NAS "is a utopian vision that describes a new era of harmony and human progress, with an emphasis on healthful living, inner peace, and respect for the planet."[10] They add that it includes obscure concepts such as "mystic crystal revelations, the planets aligning to produce harmony of the inner spirit, and liberation of the mind through holistic tranquility." Each of these concepts has their roots in Eastern religion.

The New Age Movement came to the United States with humble beginnings in the 1960's. But the practice of NAS has now infiltrated all areas of respected society. It is even invading our churches (which of course is the purpose for its inclusion in this book). At the time of this writing, as many as 12 million Americans are active New Age participants, and another 30 million consider themselves to be seriously interested. That's more than 10 percent of the U.S. population.

Its popularity really hit home with me in 2013. Our nearby small-city, Midwestern newspaper had a front page article in which a "certified hypnotherapist and light-worker" from a local "holistic center" was being interviewed. The discussion revolved around auras and chakras, key elements of occultic New Age beliefs. If that wasn't bad enough, the clients at the center during the interview happened to be a woman that I knew and her young granddaughter. I became very concerned for their spiritual health, particularly the young girl, because of how enticing these New Age concepts can be. The vulnerability of this girl, or anybody who is not well-grounded in their faith in Christ, became remarkably apparent to me with this close-to-home encounter.

Many different religions and philosophical beliefs are welcomed in New Age Spirituality, including Christianity, Eastern religions, Native American practices, and psychic phenomenon. Despite the inclusion of these multiple spiritual belief systems, NAS is really humanistic to the core. It's a belief that says we can move toward a utopian world of peace and unity rather than conflict and hatred — without God's help. It's also a belief that says we can move away from sickness and poverty toward health and prosperity for all — without God's help. And it's a belief in the potential to overcome all odds and achieve the impossible — without God's help.

USHERING IN END TIMES PROPHECY

New agers are also expecting a new world order — a coming global utopia created by a one-world government and a humanistic, unified religion. This belief is actually playing a role in fulfilling end times biblical prophecy. In Revelation 13:1-8, there is a description of the coming one-world government. The beast (Antichrist) is made its supreme leader by the dragon (Satan) during the Tribulation. In Revelation 17:1-18, a one-world religion is described as "the great prostitute." Eventually, the Antichrist will destroy this man-made religion and establish himself as god.

With these prophecies in mind, it seems quite evident that NAS is being used as a highly-successful tool of Satan. A broad-reaching mindset is being created across the earth in which people will have no trouble accepting a one-world government or religion.

A CHANGE IN PRIORITIES

While New Age Spirituality would lead you to believe that all roads lead to God, this stands in complete contradiction to Scripture. In John 14:6 Jesus said, "I am the way and the truth and the life. No one comes to the Father except through me." The ultimate appeal of NAS is that it allows for a person to be "spiritual" yet tolerant and accepting of all beliefs, with no expectation of righteousness or obedience to God. Sadly, these fleshly reasons have led many self-described Christians to participate in New Age practices while claiming to walk with Jesus.

But if a person could truly be a Christ-follower, yet still submit to New Age beliefs, it would completely change their priorities. When you believe that just about everybody is going to heaven, the thought of convincing people of their need for a savior is no longer valid. Jesus' Great Commission in Matthew 28:19-20 to "go and make disciples of all nations" becomes unnecessary. Or in Mark 16:15-16: "Go into all the world and preach the good news to all creation. Whoever believes and is baptized will be saved, but whoever does not believe will be condemned." And in Acts 1:8: "But you will receive power when the Holy Spirit comes on you; and you will be my witnesses in Jerusalem, and in all Judea and Samaria, and to the ends of the earth."

If all spiritual roads lead to heaven, then why does Jesus repeatedly, *urgently* instruct us to be witnesses for Him and His Gospel? With a New Age belief a Christian's main goal would no longer be evangelism, but instead making life better on this earth until we all reach heaven.

AN INCOMPLETE GOSPEL

As the concept of New Age Spirituality invades the Kingdom, it's easy see why the so-called "social gospel" has become so popular in many denominations. Doing the work of the Lord as found in Matthew 25 — feeding the hungry, giving water to the thirsty, providing clothes to the needy, caring for the sick, etc. — is an essential aspect of being a Christian, but it is not an end unto itself. Rather, these actions should be used as an opportunity to open doors to the real Gospel.

It is hard to hear that Jesus died for your sins when the person sharing that good news doesn't seem to care that you are struggling to put food on the table — if you have a table at all. But when you meet the needs of those who are suffering, they will be much more willing to hear what you have to say about the One who caused you to express such loving concern in the first place.

A hypothetical example may help provide greater understanding of the shortcomings of practicing a mere social gospel. Let's say there is a church that provides regular free meals to those in need. Day after day, these people come and go, and they are appreciative. And the volunteers at the church are left feeling good about showing the love of Christ to them. Unfortunately the gospel is never presented — verbally, through Christian literature, or in any other way. One night a man even reached out spiritually, asking for a Bible after a meal, but he was told they didn't have one to give him. This example is consistent with the social gospel; the physical needs are being met while the spiritual needs are largely ignored.

Obviously, this is of great concern. Taking care of the temporal needs of people is a wonderful and important aspect of being a Christian. But if the help these people receive only bridges the gap until they spend their eternity in hell, then it is clearly not sufficient. Meeting their needs has to be a means to an end; an opportunity to share the real Gospel, that through Jesus they can have their needs met forever.

Once a person trusts Christ as their Savior, then the desire to meet the needs of others should become a natural overflow of their new life as a believer. But again, it should always be done with a concerned focus on the eternal destination of the people being served. The truth is, as we saw a few moments ago in Mark 16, those who do not believe in the good news (that Jesus died on a cross and rose again as payment for sins) "will be condemned," meaning they will spend their eternity separated from God. This critical message has to be conveyed as we are ministering to the needs of others.

BELIEVER BEWARE

New Age Spirituality ultimately provides Satan with a vehicle for advancing his purposes in a non-threatening, yet insidious, way. Whole books have been written about the complexities of NAS. But as a brief tutorial, I will pass along only some of the most common words, phrases and practices as a way of raising red flags when you hear them.

Anytime people talk about gems or crystals that produce energy or power, beware. In his book *Invasion of Other Gods* Dr. David Jeremiah wrote:

"Crystals can become objects of demonic influence, just as destructive to mind and soul as magic charms or other occultic articles believed to possess supernatural power for either good or evil use. They become vehicles for spirits to work through, much like divining rods, Ouija boards, or tarot cards. The devil doesn't care whether there is anything inherent in the object at all; if he can get you to put your trust in that object; he can use it as a way to establish a beachhead in your life."[11]

Make no mistake about it. These seemingly harmless things have opened up countless people to demonic oppression and even possession.

UNHEALTHY "HEALING"

The terms "holistic health" and "homeopathic treatments" should also be viewed with caution. While these methods of medical care are not in and of themselves wrong or sinful, if they are infused with spiritual overtones that stray from biblical teaching they should be avoided. Be particularly wary if these practices are coupled with terms such as "self-realization," "self-actualization," or "enlightenment."

As New Age beliefs began to steadily infiltrate the medical field, the Christian Chiropractors Association created a policy statement to offer guidance to its members. Again in his book *Invasion of Other Gods*, Dr. David Jeremiah included this statement from the CCA:

> "In order that we might have clear discernment of Satan's deceptive methods, we adopt the following guidelines in identifying New Age healing: Healing which applies occult energies, forces, chi, yin, yang, magnetic healing, life essence, cosmic consciousness, psychic diagnosis, astrology, channeling, etc... The scriptures clearly teach against this practice."[12]

The various words and phrases used in this statement should be added to the list of those to be wary of as part of NAS.

I was recently looking through the bargain section of a major bookstore (my favorite section I might add) and ran across several books with troubling titles: *The Tai Chi Healing Bible, The Pilates Healing Bible, The Herbal Healing Bible, The Crystal Healing Bible, and The Yoga Healing Bible*. It would appear that New Age practitioners are no longer shy about expressing the belief that their version of spirituality provides a path to healing equal to what is found in the *Holy* Bible.

But the Scriptures give us clear direction on where we should place our trust. Throughout the gospels, Jesus healed people with serious diseases and even raised people from the dead. Then he said in John 14:12: "I tell you the truth, anyone who has faith in me will do what I have been doing. He will do even greater things than these, because I am going to the Father."

So we as Christians are given the great privilege of being involved in the healing process. But the important thing to note is that it is not about faith in ourselves or just any spiritual belief system, it is about faith in *Jesus*.

In a supernatural mystery, the opportunity for healing became available through His crucifixion. A messianic prophecy in Isaiah 53:5 says: "But he was pierced for our transgressions, he was crushed for our iniquities; the punishment that brought us peace was upon him, and by his wounds we are healed."

About sixty years after Jesus fulfilled this prophecy, the apostle Peter reiterated that truth in 1 Peter 2:24: "He himself bore our sins in his body on the tree, so that we might die to sins and live for righteousness; by his wounds you have been healed."

When Jesus died on a cross and rose to life again, He broke the unchecked power of sin. Sin ultimately causes death, both spiritually and physically. So Jesus' death and resurrection not only provided the opportunity for eternal spiritual healing (salvation) for those who believe, He also made provision for temporal physical healing. Therefore, the blessing that is available to us is spelled out James 5:15-16:

> And the prayer offered in faith will make the sick person well; the Lord will raise him up. If he has sinned, he will be forgiven. Therefore confess your sins to each other and pray for each other so that you may be healed. The prayer of the righteous man is powerful and effective.

This passage reinforces the spiritual principle that it is the *Lord* who will raise the sick person up, or in other words, heal them.

A PERVASIVE PRACTICE

In the last few decades there has been a practice that has moved from its roots in Eastern religion, to respectability in the West as part of New Age Spirituality, to a troubling acceptance among many who call themselves Christians. One of the reasons it has been embraced is because of its apparent ability to provide physical, mental, and even spiritual healing. This has happened despite the fact that its purpose from the start was to provide Hindus with a method of reaching a mystical union with the universal soul.

Several times when I have brought into question the acceptability of this practice in the lives of Christians, I have faced an almost indescribable resistance; usually not harsh or argumentative like someone slamming a door in your face or yelling "shut up!", but more like someone hanging up the phone on a telemarketer. It's like they're saying, "I don't want what you are selling so I'm not going to listen. Even if the 'product' you are trying to sell may have great value, I don't want to hear what you have to say."

The staunch loyalty that many people have developed for this practice reveals to me that it has taken on a godlike quality in their lives. (I will make a defense of this statement later in the chapter.) Because of this, perhaps many of you will be tempted to close this book now and not read what I have to say. But please "don't hang up!" I guarantee what I have to "sell" is valuable and worth your time.

Perhaps by now you've figured out that I am talking about yoga. It is a 2,000-year-old Hindu practice designed for a specific religious purpose. This is made clear in the Sanskrit definition of the word: "yolk or union" with god. Yoga was created by a guru named Patanjali. Through gazing upon certain symbols and reciting certain sacred sounds or mantras (such as the well-known "Om"), an individual supposedly approaches mystical union with the universal soul. That was the created goal of yoga — to divorce oneself from the material world and unite with the impersonal cosmic god of the universe. This ultimately allows the Hindu to finally escape the cycle of reincarnation.

Kundalini, considered the "mother" of all forms of yoga, is a method by which divine energy thought to reside as a coiled serpent at the base of the spine is aroused through physical and breathing exercises. This serpent ascends through six chakras in the spine and aims for union with a Hindu deity in a seventh chakra located in the crown of the head. From there, a person can move from a mostly physical experience to a more spiritual experience.

Through meditation on a mantra, they call upon the Hindu deity to aid them in transcendence. According to one modern day guru, this creates a "new man" who "is happily mindless." But emptying the mind in such a way puts out a "vacancy" sign, making the person vulnerable to satanic attack (Matthew 12:43-45). This has led to many documented cases of demon possession or insanity.

A SUBTLE INTRODUCTION TO HINDUISM

Yoga has become very mainstream in western culture in recent years, thanks in large part to a boost in its credibility through New Age Spirituality. As of this writing, 16.5 million Americans practice it regularly with widespread acceptance in public schools, health care, the workplace, and even in many churches.

It is commonly said by well-meaning individuals that they only do yoga for the exercise. But is that possible? Remember, the definition of yoga is "yolk or union" with god. According to Patanjali, even the postures and breathing in yoga are a spiritual expression. The ancient gurus actually developed the postures, or asanas, to prepare the body for meditation; when you can control the body, you can control the mind. In *The Complete Bible Answer Book*, Hank Hanegraaff wrote:

> "Coupled with breathing exercises and meditation practices, asana positions are the pathway to serenity and

spirituality...While multitudes are being seduced into believing that asanas are spiritually neutral, nothing could be farther from the truth."[13]

The breathing techniques in yoga, known as pranayama, were developed to purify and remove distractions from the mind to make it easier to concentrate and meditate. The gurus taught that a life force or energy exists everywhere and flows through each of us through the breath. That is why the breathing techniques were made such a major focus of the yoga experience.

So the physical practices of yoga were meant from the start to be a preparation for the spiritual aspect, reaching out to the universal soul or cosmic consciousness. And despite what many believe today, the effects of the physical often inadvertently translate into the spiritual. Again in *The Complete Bible Answer Book*, Hanegraaff wrote:

"In sum, while an alarming number of Western Christians suppose they can achieve physical and spiritual well-being through a form of yoga divorced from its Eastern worldview, in reality attempts to Christianize Hinduism only Hinduize Christianity."[14]

WISE WORDS OF WARNING

There was a time a few years ago that I became very concerned about the growing acceptance of yoga among Christians. Certain brothers and sisters in Christ who I truly respected didn't seem to have any problem with it. Then a Christian evangelist who grew up and ministers in India, the epicenter of Hinduism, came to a church in our area. It gave me the opportunity to ask him, "Is there any validity to my concern about yoga invading the Church, or is it just a fear based on incorrect information?"

His response was indirect, and yet very direct, at the same time. He said, "Let me put it this way: Christians in India do not practice yoga." In just those few words, he said believers in

Christ who know the real truth about yoga *will not* allow it to be a part of their lives.

Christian author and filmmaker Caryl Matrisciana was also born and raised in India. The promotional announcement for her 2008 documentary *Yoga Uncoiled* included these words: "Many believe they can practice yoga postures, breathing, and focusing techniques devoid of yoga's spirituality, not realizing that yoga is an inherent part of Hindu philosophy which teaches man and nature are one with divinity."

Christians generally practice hatha yoga, which is commonly looked at as mere exercise without the spiritual element. But in a *Christ in Prophecy* TV broadcast from August 2011, Matrisciana said, "In Hindu teaching, it is known that there is no yoga without Hinduism and no Hinduism without yoga. The two cannot be separated."

Even the most innocent ventures into the practice of yoga have been known to leave people vulnerable to demonic spiritual activity. Chris Lawson is director of the Spiritual Research Network. In his July 2008 website article "Kundalini Energy: Yoga's Power, Influence and Occult Phenomena in the Church" Lawson wrote:

"Whether one is just a beginner or an expert, all yoga postures and breath prayers have the capacity to invoke dark, evil powers. Involving oneself with yoga...and any form of kundalini energy arousal can lead to severe and prolonged bouts of demonic oppression, mental states of extreme depression and despondency, demonic entities influencing the human body, etc. I have personally seen and helped Christians that have been left in vegetable-like mental states and who have experienced undiagnosable excruciating pain."

Perhaps it would be beneficial to read Mr. Lawson's statement again. He mentions several frightening manifestations of demonic activity in the lives of many, many people — including

Christians — as a result of their association with yoga. This is not child's play, and it points to the main reason for this conversation about yoga. Is it an acceptable practice for believers in Christ?

Even with so-called "Christian" yoga, it would seem from the aforementioned research and testimonials that it is not likely one can completely divorce the spiritual aspect of yoga from the beneficial exercise. Even if it were possible, what about others who are drawn to yoga by our endorsement as Christians? It is an extremely valid concern that these people could end up with a teacher — or in a setting — that makes no effort to guard against the mystical aspects of yoga which can open the door to demonic activity.

HARRY POTTER: HARMLESS OR HEINOUS?

I have heard Christian advocates for yoga say, "I have been practicing it for years and have not had any associated negative experiences." This is undoubtedly true for most yoga enthusiasts. But I like to draw a comparison between yoga and another popular modern spectacle that has occultic roots — the Harry Potter phenomenon.

When the book and eventual movie series first burst onto the scene in 1999, there were actually many well-known Christians who defended it, despite its repeated references to witches, warlocks, incantations, spells, and other occultic practices that call on the power of Satan for supernatural abilities. Many later changed their minds after seeing the impact the series was having on the popularity of Witchcraft.

What yoga has been to Hinduism, Harry Potter has been to Witchcraft. Both have been naively accepted as harmless, while they have exposed millions to the dangers of the occult.

According to figures compiled by Walter Martin, Jill Martin Rische, and Kurt Van Gorden in their book *The Kingdom of the Occult*, in 1990 — nearly a decade before Harry Potter was introduced — the number of practicing witches in the U.S. was estimated to be no more than 65 thousand. In 2007, not quite a decade after Harry Potter became popular, the estimate had skyrocketed to anywhere from 200 thousand to 600 thousand.[15] While this is a broad estimate, it still shows that at the very least there has been a three-fold increase in the number of people practicing Witchcraft since the series captivated the nation.

A PERILOUS IMPACT

Once Harry Potter started to become a household name in the U.S. and around the world, organizations and websites related to Witchcraft began to see a many-fold increase in the number of people wanting to learn more about the practice. A Barna Group survey released in May 2006 even found that one in eight teenagers said they wanted to learn more about Witchcraft as a result of their exposure to the Harry Potter chronicles.

Now I have talked to more than one Christian parent who told me their child read the Harry Potter books and it has had no effect on them. Therefore, they see no problem with it. And my response has been "Praise the Lord" because their son or daughter is apparently among the seven in eight who were apparently not so negatively affected.

Those odds seem pretty good, right? But consider this. Let's say there was a youth evangelist holding a major stadium crusade in which eighty thousand teenagers showed up. At the end, the evangelist gave an altar call and ten thousand of those young people went forward to receive Christ, or to further explore what Christianity is all about. We would say that was a highly-successful outreach for the Lord and would be absolutely thrilled at the result. Others would want to model their ministries after this event because of its extraordinary success. A quick check of the math shows that this would be one in eight teens who were drawn to Christ through the crusade.

Even though this is a fictional event, the Harry Potter impact sadly is not. It would be hard to find a better "evangelical" effort for Witchcraft and the occult than the Harry Potter series. So why,

why would we as Christians want to endorse such things, let alone introduce them into the lives of those we love and care about?

The same can be said for the subject that started this conversation. I have not seen any statistics, but for the sake of argument let's just say that, similar to the Harry Potter impact, only one in eight Christians who practice yoga actually experience any negative spiritual side-effects such as those we saw in the previously mentioned testimonials. Then it would make sense that the large majority of people who practice so-called "Christian" yoga would say they have no problem with it. But it would be hard to find a better "evangelical" effort for Eastern religion and the occult than yoga. So why, *why* would we as Christians want to endorse such a practice, let alone introduce it into the lives of those we love and care about?

CONCLUDING THOUGHT

The Bible says Satan is like a lion prowling around looking for someone to devour (1 Peter 5:8). When we introduce Eastern religions, New Age Spirituality, and dark "evangelistic" tools such as yoga and Harry Potter into our lives we are effectively allowing Satan an opportunity to pounce. These spiritual beliefs and their related practices have occultic roots. When combined with a modern naivete about their potential dangers, they clearly provide just the opening Satan needs to rip apart and "devour" an unsuspecting life.

My encouragement would be to forsake anything that can introduce the powers of darkness into your life or the lives of those you care about. There are plenty of safe alternatives to yoga, Harry Potter, or anything else involving questionable spirituality. And when you are seeking physical or mental healing and hope, put all of the idols aside and chase after the one true God — the God of the Bible. No matter how popular these other things may become in the culture, the potential for spiritual damage — now and forever — is just not worth it.

11–THE BROAD ROAD: MORMONISM & THE JEHOVAH'S WITNESSES

They say their beliefs are based at least in part on the Bible.
But what they believe and what the Scriptures teach have
only a passing similarity.

In 2012 the Republican presidential candidate was Mitt Romney, a man who professed his faith as a Mormon. His high-profile campaign took what had been a rather quiet discussion into a national debate: Is Mormonism part of true Christianity? A well-known pastor was asked that question on nationwide television and he replied, "In my mind they are." He mentioned that Romney had proclaimed Jesus to be his Savior and Lord so that was good enough for him. When the interviewer brought up the differences between Mormon and Christian beliefs, the pastor responded, "I'm not one to judge the little details of it."

This pastor may have been influenced by New Age thinking because, during the same election cycle, he said in another nationwide TV interview that about 90 percent of people in the United States are Christians. This certainly contradicts the biblical truth that is our current focus from Matthew 7:13: "...broad is the road that leads to destruction, and many enter through it." It also disputes the word of the American people themselves. In an ABC News poll from January 2006, 83 percent of U.S. citizens claimed to be Christian. Just under seven years later, a December 2006 Gallup poll found that only 77 percent of Americans identified themselves as Christian.

This chapter will deal with a couple of prominent religions whose followers would claim in such a poll to be Christians. But we will see from their doctrines it is simply not correct to claim that title, regardless of what people like this well-known pastor say. I call them "pseudo-Christian" religions because they say their beliefs are based at least in part on the Bible. But what they believe and what the Scriptures teach have only a passing similarity. The "little details of it" are actually, again, irreconcilable differences. What this pastor said when he had a prominent, national platform was troubling evidence of a false belief that has invaded the Kingdom, and the record must be set straight so others aren't led astray down the broad road.

After discussing Romney, it seems only fitting that we look at Mormonism first. It has grown into the largest and fastest growing pseudo-Christian religion in the world, with about 11 million members as of this writing, and about 300 thousand converts a year. This has a lot to do with the fact that Mormons emphasize missions to their children almost from birth. And once a Mormon teen graduates from high school, they are told it is their duty to serve a two-year missionary term.

Mormons call themselves The Church of Jesus Christ of Latter-Day Saints, so even their name feeds the perception that they are truly born-again believers. Despite this, a major focus of their missions effort is among those who already call themselves Christians. Why would this be if Mormons are actually fellow believers? In fact, it is estimated that three-quarters of all new Mormon converts had a previous Christian affiliation.

MORMONISM: A BRIEF HISTORY

Mormonism is a comparatively young religion. It was founded by a 15-year-old named Joseph Smith in 1820. While praying in the woods near his home in upstate New York, Smith says he received a vision of God the Father and God the Son. They told him that the existing denominations were all wrong, a new church was needed, and that he would lead it. In 1823, Smith claimed the angel Moroni appeared and told him there was a book buried near his home inscribed on gold plates. It took three years before Moroni would reveal where the plates were buried.

Smith said he began translating the "reformed Egyptian hieroglyphics" on the gold plates by using a seer stone found with the plates. They supposedly contained a historical record about two ancient civilizations that inhabited the Americas, along with the true gospel. The gold plates were said to be written by the angel Moroni's father, the prophet Mormon; hence the name, the *Book of Mormon.*

Despite much opposition, by 1844 Smith managed to gain a significant number of followers in Illinois, Missouri, and Ohio. He even became mayor of Nauvoo, Illinois. While there, Smith continued to come up with new "revelations" — including a doctrine that allowed for polygamy. This was largely the cause of Smith's undoing. He had more than thirty wives, and other Mormons reported in a newspaper that gross immorality was taking place among church leaders. This allegedly included underage girls. Smith and some of his loyal followers tried to destroy the newspaper office and he was arrested. Soon after, a mob broke into the jail and Smith was killed.

A Mormon apostle, Brigham Young, then took over leadership. In order to avoid persecution, Young led the church faithful westward in 1847. Their journey ended at the Great Salt Lake in Utah where Young established a Mormon settlement — Salt Lake City.

Interestingly, just as polygamy was the undoing of Joseph Smith, it almost brought an end to Mormonism itself. The practice continued until 1890, at which time the U.S. government threatened to shut down the church and deny statehood to Utah if the polygamy didn't stop. So the fourth president of the Mormon Church, Wilford Woodruff, called for an end to the practice.

Mormonism survived, and to this day the church is headquartered in Salt Lake City and is the dominant religion in the state of Utah.

A FANTASTIC FRAUD

It's hard to sugarcoat the facts when it comes to Mormonism. Joseph Smith had a fertile imagination and was no doubt a very charismatic man. There was no way to disprove his claims at the time he started the religion, but modern evidences have proved the fraudulent nature of most of his writings.

For example, the *Book of Mormon* supposedly contains a history of how the Native American people came to be established in the Western Hemisphere. They were purported to be descendants of the biblical Jews. Yet modern DNA samples taken from Indian tribes in North, Central, and South America have uncovered virtually no Jewish blood, but rather, a highly-predominant Asian ancestry. In addition, no archeological or cultural evidence has ever been found that would corroborate the ancient civilizations described in the *Book of Mormon.*

Mormon anthropologist and scholar Thomas Murphy admitted as much in the 2003 documentary *DNA vs. The Mormon Church* produced by Living Hope Christian Fellowship of Brigham City, Utah. Murphy said most Mormon scholars agree that the American Indians could not possibly be descendents of Hebrews (called Lamanites in the Book of Mormon). He said that would be "genetically, archeologically, historically, and linguistically impossible." Keep in mind this was coming from someone who still considered himself to be a Mormon. Simply put, these facts show the *Book of Mormon* to be an elaborate fraud.

Three years after Smith concocted the *Book of Mormon* he wrote the *Book of Commandments*. Then after two more years, that book was substantially revised and renamed *Doctrines and Covenants*. It includes many of the well-known Mormon doctrines such as eternal progression, polygamy, and the ability of humans to become gods. (We'll look at these in more detail in a moment.)

The *Pearl of Great Price* was also written by Smith. Among other things, it contains Smith's translation of the so-called Book of Moses and Gospel of Matthew. Portions were supposedly translated by Smith from scrolls found with Egyptian mummies that he purchased from a traveling antiquities salesman in 1835. He claimed they were writings of the patriarchal Abraham. Thus, Smith called them the Book of Abraham.

But modern day Egyptologists, who were not available on the North American continent at that time, have determined that the scrolls were not scriptural writings at all. They were in reality just remnants of common Egyptian funeral texts and related drawings one would expect to find encased with mummies. This indisputable fact shows the *Pearl of Great Price* to be another elaborate fraud birthed in Smith's cunning and creative mind.

Smith also created his own version of the Bible, the "Inspired Version," as he claimed every other translation was corrupt. Even though he did not know Hebrew, Aramaic, or Greek (the original languages of the Bible) he made thousands of changes to the King James Version. It should come as no surprise that this translation included a passage in Genesis 50 predicting the coming of none other than Joseph Smith himself.

A GROWING NUMBER OF GODS

Since Mormons believe that all Christian denominations have corrupted beliefs, they would argue that wherever the doctrines differ, the non-Mormons are the ones who have it wrong. But hopefully it is clear by now that Mormonism lacks any credibility even before we compare its beliefs with those of Christianity, particularly since the Mormon doctrines are based on fraudulently produced "holy books."

Among the most glaring differences has to do with their belief in eternal progression. Mormons believe that Father God, who rules the earth today, was once a man who became a god. Father God was conceived by another god who existed before him, who was conceived by another god who existed before him, etc. Just as the current Father God descended from an eternal progression of other gods, faithful Mormons believe that they too can eventually become gods.

In contrast, the Bible teaches that God is the one and only eternal being who had no beginning and has no end. Psalm 90:2 says, "...from everlasting to everlasting you are God." "Everlasting" is translated from the Hebrew word *olam*, which speaks in terms of an endless existence in time. In other words, God was not conceived; He has always existed.

In Isaiah 45:5, God Himself speaks through the prophet saying, "I am the Lord, and there is no other; apart from me there is no God." And again in Isaiah 46:9: "I am God, and there is no other; I am God, and there is none like me." These verses completely and directly contradict the Mormon doctrine which says our current Father God is just one of many.

SUPERNATURAL SIBLING RIVALRY

The Mormon belief about Jesus is also dramatically different from what the Bible teaches. They believe the current Father God grew up as a man on another planet and then became God of earth. He and Mother God had millions of spirit children together. Their firstborn was Jesus, followed by Lucifer. (Yes, Jesus and Satan are spirit brothers according to Mormon doctrine.) Jesus was chosen by Father God to be the savior of the other spirit children who populated the earth. When this happened, Lucifer became so angry that he rebelled and was banished to earth.

Most Mormons believe the spirit child Jesus was introduced to the earth as a human after Father God had a sexual relationship with Mary. Jesus then grew up, got married (to perhaps more than one wife), and had several children. Jesus died on a cross, was resurrected with a new body, and returned to heaven. He is now waiting to replace the current Father God when he moves on, or progresses, to an even greater realm.

Mormons teach that each person born on earth was once a spirit child in heaven and we all have the opportunity to follow the pattern of Jesus, and Father God before him. By being faithful Mormons, people can progress toward godhood and then have spirit children of their own. These children will eventually be born on a planet and the cycle repeats.

In contrast, as we saw in the chapter on Satan earlier in this book, the Bible tells us that Lucifer was in reality a spirit being created by God along with the other angels before the earth was formed. He rebelled against God and was cast out of heaven. Jesus on the other hand is part of the triune Godhead; the Father, the Son, and the Holy Spirit. In John 1:1-3, we see that Jesus (the Word) has always existed:

> In the beginning was the Word, and the Word was with God, and the Word was God. He was with God in the beginning. Through him all things were made; without him nothing was made that has been made.

This is completely contradictory to Mormon doctrine which proclaims Lucifer (Satan) and Jesus to be spirit brothers who had a falling out because of some sort of cosmic sibling rivalry.

The Bible teaches that Jesus was not introduced to the earth through a bizarre sexual encounter between Father God and Mary, but rather, as the Holy Spirit supernaturally made Mary pregnant while she was still a virgin (Luke 1:35). And after He grew to be a man, we are never told in the Scriptures of any romantic relationship that Jesus may have had, let alone any marriage or children. It would escape reason to believe that such important facts would have been ignored by all of the gospel writers. Yet this is part of Mormon doctrine.

INNOCENT SINFULNESS

Mormons believe that, since all people were once spirit children, they are innocent at birth. So anytime a sin is committed it is viewed as a mistake or an act of ignorance. Mormons are taught that they will be resurrected after death thanks to Jesus' example, but His sacrifice is not what saves them. As we will see in a moment, *all* people are saved eventually based on their level of good works and the extent to which they follow the beliefs of the Mormon Church.

The Bible on the other hand teaches that man is born into sin and is prone to rebellion toward God. In Romans 5:12, Paul describes the original sin of man through Adam and its impact on humanity: "...sin entered the world through one man, and death through sin, and in this way death came to all men, because all sinned..."

Paul was recounting what happened at the dawn of human history some four thousand years earlier, when Adam was instructed by God in Genesis 2:17 not to eat from the tree of the knowledge of good and evil. The serpent, which was indwelt by Satan, tempted Adam through his wife Eve. In blatant rebellion against God and His command, Adam ate fruit from the tree in Genesis 3:6. But as Romans 5 continues, Paul explains that even though sin and death entered the world through one man — Adam — atonement and eternal life also became available through one man — Jesus Christ.

ETERNITY: IT'S ALL GOOD

This leads us to the final irreconcilable difference I'd like to highlight between Mormonism and Christianity — the destination of believers after they die. Mormons teach that there are three heavens — the celestial, the terrestrial, and the telestial. In simple terms, the celestial heaven is the greatest, reserved for only the faithful Mormons. After that comes the terrestrial heaven, where the less-than-faithful Mormons and some exceptional non-Mormons go. The telestial heaven is set aside for the non-Mormons who have been mostly bad. Before entering this heaven, these people must suffer temporarily in hell; a kind of prison sentence for their crimes. There is no eternal punishment in Mormon doctrine.

Conversely, the Bible teaches that there is only one eternal home for faithful believers, the new heaven and new earth as found in Revelation 21. Once there, John describes in verse 3 what he sees in his prophetic vision — the blessed hope that awaits Christ-followers:

> And I heard a loud voice from the throne saying, "Now the dwelling of God is with men, and he will live with them. They will be his people, and God himself will be with them and will be their God."

In total contrast to this perfectly glorious moment, those who reject God to the end will spend their eternity in the place of torment called hell. In 2 Thessalonians 1:8-9 Paul writes:

> He will punish those who do not obey the gospel of our Lord Jesus. They will be punished with everlasting destruction and shut out from the presence of the Lord and from the majesty of His power...

This and the other doctrines we have discussed vary dramatically between Mormonism and Christianity. To believe that the same God came up with these completely contradictory messages is just not reasonable. The vast differences clearly indicate that Mormonism is not a Christian denomination at all, but merely another false religion being used by Satan to deceive millions into a hopeless eternity separated from God.

JEHOVAH'S WITNESSES: A BRIEF HISTORY

There is one other pseudo-Christian religion that I want to look at because of its growing influence in the United States and around the world. Similar to Mormonism, the Jehovah's Witnesses are showing steady growth because of their aggressive evangelism techniques. Many a joke has been told about the well-known door-to-door visits paid by the JW faithful, but their success is not a laughing matter. On average, a Jehovah's Witness spends about ten hours each month visiting homes sharing their version of truth. As a result, converts are gained at a rate of about 55 hundred each week.

The religion was founded by Charles T. Russell in 1872 when he was twenty years old, although it wasn't called the Jehovah's Witnesses just yet. Russell encountered some Seventh Day Adventists, a group formed about a decade earlier by former followers of William Miller. Miller had twice incorrectly predicted when Christ would return to establish his millennial kingdom on the earth. Although Miller was discredited, the Seventh Day Adventists continued a focus on predicting Christ's return which captivated Russell.

He began the International Bible Students' Association, which was renamed Zion's Watchtower Tract Society in 1881, and printed the first edition of *The Watchtower* magazine. Russell made his own prediction — that Christ would return in 1914. Obviously that didn't happen, but Jehovah's Witnesses saved face by pointing out that a history-changing event began that year — World War I.

Russell's religious movement continued to grow until his death in 1916. He was succeeded by Joseph Rutherford who introduced another magazine, *The Golden Age*, which is now called *Awake*. He added radio broadcasts to the evangelistic efforts in the 1920's, and began calling the movement The Jehovah's Witnesses in 1931.

Rutherford died in 1942 and Nathan Knorr took over leadership of the religion. During his tenure, Knorr established a training school for missionaries and the Jehovah's Witnesses grew from about 115 thousand to over two million by 1977. The growth has continued. As of this writing, there are more than six million Jehovah's Witnesses in 230 countries, including about 988 thousand in the United States.

A BELITTLED BIBLE

Similar to Mormons, the Jehovah's Witnesses accept the Bible as Holy Scripture, but only *their* version of the Bible. The New World Translation is similar to but different from historically-accepted

Bible translations. Also like the Mormons, JW's believe they alone have the correct interpretation of the Scriptures. The foundational doctrines of the Jehovah's Witnesses come from a seven-volume series penned by Charles Russell called Studies in the Scriptures. In one of the most obvious of red flags when identifying a false religion, Russell told his followers that these writings would be more important to read than the Bible itself.

This troubling concept carries on as other doctrines and witnessing guidelines continue to be taught through *The Watchtower* and *Awake* magazines. To this day, the content found in the regular editions of *The Watchtower* is viewed by JW's as if it were biblical doctrine.

A TRIVIALIZED TRINITY

As with the other false religions we have discussed, there are irreconcilable differences between the doctrines believed by Jehovah's Witnesses and those taught in the Bible. Among them is what they believe about God, Jesus, and the Holy Spirit. JW's are taught that there is no Trinity. They believe God has one name, Jehovah. Jesus is not the son of God, but rather, Michael the archangel. Michael was called Jesus when he came to earth. He died on a stake, not a cross, and after his resurrection he returned to heaven and resumed his role as Michael the archangel. Similarly, Jehovah's Witnesses believe the Holy Spirit is not part of the Godhead, but rather, an active force. (You might notice their understanding of the Holy Spirit fits very nicely with New Age beliefs.)

While the word "Trinity" is not found in the Bible, the reality of a triune God is. For example, the plural Hebrew word "Elohim" is used to describe God in various Old Testament passages such as Genesis 1:26: "Then God said, 'Let *us* make man in *our* image, in *our* likeness...'" (Emphasis added)

This makes no sense unless God exists as a plurality. There are various passages of Scripture describing each person of the Trinity as God, but I'll share just those that to me are the most simple and clear.

- As relates to the Father, Romans 1:7 says: "Grace and peace to you from God our Father..."

- Describing Jesus as God incarnate, Colossians 2:9 says: "For in Christ all the fullness of the Deity lives in bodily form."

- And the Holy Spirit is revealed as God in Acts 5:3-4: "Then Peter said, 'Ananias, how is it that Satan has so filled your heart that you have lied to the Holy Spirit...What made you think of doing such a thing? You have not lied to men but to God.'"

So the Father, the Son, and the Holy Spirit together make up the Trinity. There is no question that understanding a three-in-one God is difficult, if not impossible. But I came to a clearer understanding of the concept one time when I was listening to a performance by a very skilled men's trio. Individually these men were extremely talented and their music was a delight to hear. But put them together and the result was remarkable. Each man had a different role in the trio, yet their unique voices meshed together to create something even more amazing than they were able to produce alone. This to me was a picture of the Trinity; three distinct and dynamic persons with different roles harmonizing into one glorious all-powerful, all-knowing, ever-present God.

SALVATION: NOT A LOT AT STAKE

The Jehovah's Witnesses understanding about salvation varies greatly from biblical teaching as well. Since they do not believe Jesus is the son of God, JW's are taught that his death on a stake only canceled out Adam's sin. This did however remove the curse of original sin, which allows them to achieve their own salvation. This happens by being faithful to the requirements of the Jehovah's Witnesses, including the well-known door-to-door witnessing, which explains at least in part their passion for this type of evangelism.

The Bible on the other hand teaches salvation is all about Jesus; that only His sacrificial death on a cross provided the opportunity for mankind to have eternal life. It is the grace of God that makes this possible through our faith in Jesus Christ — not by anything we have done. Our good works then are merely an overflow of our transformed lives (Ephesians 2:8-10).

Jehovah's Witnesses also deny the existence of hell. They believe that all non-JW's evaporate after death. But a glorious afterlife awaits the faithful Jehovah's Witnesses. There is an elite ruling class of 144 thousand who gain admittance to heaven. This is known as the Heavenly Hope. The remaining JW's will live on a new and improved earth as part of a millennial kingdom. This is called the Earthly Hope. Witnesses who have already died will remain in an unconscious state until they are resurrected in the millennium.

This doctrine is loosely based on the passage found in Revelation 21 which describes a new heaven and new earth, although it actually has been modified from original JW teaching. At the start, followers were told that only 144 thousand people would go to heaven; the faithful Jehovah's witnesses. But as their numbers surpassed that total, a new doctrine was necessary — hence the newly-created division between the elite and common classes.

A quick check of the actual wording in Revelation 21 shows the new heaven and new earth to be a combined destination; the place where faithful believers will dwell with God forever. Those who reject Him to the end will spend their eternity in the place of torment called hell.

From this examination of a few key Jehovah's Witnesses beliefs, it should be obvious that they are not at all Christian. The vast differences between their doctrines and what is taught in the Bible make any realistic attempt to reconcile the two a practice in futility.

CONCLUDING THOUGHT

It's interesting to note that both the Mormons and Jehovah's Witnesses regularly target Christians in their evangelistic efforts. This should be a clear indication of the dark origins of these religions. I believe they were created by Satan — the angel of light and father of lies — to cause confusion among sincere seekers of truth, ultimately drawing some believers of Jesus Christ and countless others away from the true Gospel. Sadly, Satan has succeeded through these false religions in leading millions into a hopeless eternity separated from God.

Neither Mormons nor Jehovah's Witnesses believe that Jesus is the one and only son of God, or that He died on a cross as a payment for their sins before He rose to life again. That means, by the Bible's definition, these people have not yet received salvation.

I encourage all Christians to have great compassion on anyone caught up in a false belief system. Show them the love of Christ at every opportunity and share your faith whenever possible. They have been deceived into a prison that will lead to an eternal death sentence unless they believe in the real Gospel and repent of their sins. They will then receive the ultimate parole through the blood of Jesus.

12–THE NARROW GATE: JESUS

Despite what is believed by so many people in this post-modern culture, the way to heaven is truly that narrow. The blood of Jesus, the perfect Lamb of God, provides the only way to salvation.

In 1999 when I was blessed to return to Christian radio after eight years away, our family had to move northward to central Minnesota. My wife and I bought an old farmhouse that we really loved, but it did not yet have an adjacent garage. The brutal winters in that area made having a shelter for our vehicles almost a necessity. With limited resources, I took on the task of building one myself with the help of a good friend and co-worker named Tom. Or more correctly, Tom took on the task of building the garage with my help. He was one of those people who had a special aptitude for being able to repair or build just about anything. Once the cement floor was laid down, we got to work.

Tom had a family of his own, so he would do as much as he could each day before he had to go home and then gave me instructions on how to proceed with the next step. There were some troubling moments at the start, such as when part of the first framed-in wall, standing by itself, blew over in a strong wind.

Then later, after the entire garage was framed in, we had another very windy day. For lack of a better word, the garage was "wiggling" in the stormy gusts and I was concerned the whole thing was going to blow over. If it had been just one wall it certainly would have collapsed, such as happened previously, but all of the walls put together made the structure just strong enough to withstand the heavy winds. Later, after the OSB boards were attached to the walls and the roof was added using the apt-ly-named hurricane clips, the entirety of the garage became so strong that it would conceivably take something like a tornado to knock it down (we don't have hurricanes in Minnesota).

This is similar to how I would describe what has happened over the years with my faith in Jesus Christ. Early on as my Christian beliefs were being framed in, I was rather fragile and the winds of life were able to blow me from time to time off of my solid foundation. Later as I began to take on some spiritual maturity, my faith could still be shaken when life became stormy and a collapse remained a possibility. But in recent years, my faith has become more complete and I have become solidly con-vinced that Jesus Christ and the absolute truth of the Bible can be fully trusted and believed. None of the hurricane-force winds of life could convince me otherwise.

Earlier in this book, I shared many of the reasons for my confidence in the inerrancy and infallibility of God's Word, and I have found that its truths continue to be revealed and proven in my own life. That's why, when the Bible says that Jesus is the only way to salvation, I believe it without hesitation. The remainder of this book will be my attempt to help you "finish your garage" so that you too can become absolutely certain of this truth.

THERE'S POWER IN HIS NAME

Just the name of Jesus has the ability to bring strong reaction, whether good or bad. Reflecting how difficult it is to understand or describe this truth, an old Bill Gaither Trio song says, "Jesus, there's just something about that name." When the mere name of Jesus is mentioned, Christians raise their hands in worship and demons have to flee.

It's interesting that prayers which have been allowed for a couple of centuries in the United States — such as when politicians meet, or in schools at the start of the day or before their sporting events — now often face the court-ordered requirement that the name of Jesus can't be mentioned. Why would this be unless there is something special and unique about that name?

There is tremendous power in the name of Jesus that can even change nations. Look at what happens in areas of the world where His name is not honored. Communist countries such as China, North Korea, Cuba, Venezuela, and the former Soviet Union just to name a few, are places where atheism has been taught and encouraged. In these countries the rights of average citizens have been minimal, and there have been many documented cases of injustices and atrocities far beyond the scope of what we can comprehend in a Judeo-Christian culture such as the United States.

As I mentioned in an earlier chapter, Muslims believe Jesus was a prophet but do not revere Him as the Son of God. Therefore, I believe it is no coincidence that Muslim-dominant countries show very little regard for human rights. This is particularly true when it comes to religious rights, where those who do not proclaim allegiance to Islam face anything from oppressive taxes, to imprisonment, to death.

During World War II, the Nazis effectively bullied the Christian church in Germany into silence, marginalizing their influence. Many pastors willingly went along with the new laws of the land, even when they went against the laws of God (a chilling trend that is now being seen at times in the twenty-first century United States). Others, such as Dietrich Bonhoeffer, stood strong on the Word of God and were martyred for their faith. The result was a ruthless military regime which was responsible for millions of deaths, including some six million Jews.

The brutality of the Japanese military was also well-documented. Shintoism is the main religion in Japan, and their emperor during World War II was largely believed to be a god. In service to the emperor, the lives of the enemy took on very little value.

A prime example was what has become known as the Bataan Death March which took place on a Philippine island in April 1942. Approximately 75 thousand Filipino and American POW's were forced by their Japanese captors to walk some sixty-five miles over several days to a prison camp in oppressive heat. They were given very little food or water. Some were beaten, shot, or bayoneted when they fell behind. Others died of exhaustion or disease. The death toll was believed to be about three thousand during the march, while more than twenty-seven thousand others died after reaching the prison camps as a result their merciless treatment.

The lives of the Japanese people themselves were also viewed as having very little value. As an example, military pilots known as kamikazes would be assigned to fly their explosives-laden planes into enemy ships at sea, taking their own lives in the process. When the name of Jesus is not revered in a country, it can become a very dark place indeed.

By the way, some still question why it is was not considered a war crime for the U.S. to drop atomic bombs on Hiroshima and Nagasaki which killed hundreds-of-thousands of Japanese civilians. It must be understood that since their leader was believed to be a god, the Japanese largely had the understanding that they could not lose and would never surrender. Taking all things into consideration, U.S. military leaders and President Harry Truman decided it would take the shock and awe of a nuclear blast to bring Japan to its knees.

They still did not surrender after Hiroshima. It took the second bomb on Nagasaki for the Japanese to come to the realization they were not divinely led and protected. They finally surrendered. In retrospect, it is truly believed by most military strategists that dropping the bombs was the most humane option for both sides. It undoubtedly saved many times the number of lives — including soldiers and civilians — over the option of a traditional military invasion of Japan that could have lasted for many years.

It is also interesting to note that the United States aided both Germany and Japan in recovery efforts after the war was over. This U.S. military philosophy — "To Liberate, Not to Conquer" — continues to this day, as we have seen in Muslim-dominant countries such as Iraq and Afghanistan. From the time our military successfully invaded these previously oppressed countries, there has been an attempt to aid the citizens in developing safe, thriving democracies with new leadership. Unfortunately, this hasn't worked as well as it did following World War II. Among other things, the dynamics of Islamic thought — which do not reconcile well with democracy — and the sectarian divisions within the religion have made success elusive.

Such merciful actions by a conquering nation are rare in human history. It has been more common to oppress, enslave, or commit genocide against the citizens of a defeated country. But the United States, driven by our Judeo-Christian values, has shown compassion for these conquered people. Is it a coincidence that Jesus said in Luke 6:27, "Love your enemies, do good to those who hate you..."? I think not. And even though it is sadly changing in our postmodern culture, it appears evident that the words of Jesus are still lingering as a driving force behind our actions as a nation.

THERE'S POWER IN HIS BLOOD

Not only is there power in the *name* of Jesus, but there is also tremendous power in the *blood* of Jesus. Only His blood has the ability to change lives for now *and* for eternity. Before Jesus came to earth in the flesh, the Old Testament Jewish priests used a sacrificial system to atone for (or cover over) the sins of the people through the blood of animals. In Leviticus 17:11, God said to Moses:

> For the life of the creature is in the blood, and I have given it to you to make atonement for yourselves on the altar; it is the blood that makes atonement for one's life.

These animals had to be without any blemish or defects. But this was only a temporary system that had to be repeated over and over. When Jesus died on a cross, the blood He shed as the perfect, sinless "Lamb of God" provided a permanent sacrifice. That made atonement for sins a possibility for all of mankind for all of eternity. This difference is described in Hebrews 10:11-12:

> Day after day every priest stands and performs his religious duties; again and again he offers the same sacrifices, which can never take away sins. But when this priest [Jesus] had offered for all time one sacrifice for sins, he sat down at the right hand of God.

In God's design, there is saving power in the blood. We see an example of this in the Passover as described in Exodus 12. God was going to inflict a final plague upon Egypt so their leader, the Pharaoh, would free the country's Jewish slaves. The first-born Egyptian people and animals would all be killed, but God instructed the Hebrews to put the blood of perfect, spotless lambs on the doorframes of their houses. God said he would pass over these homes when he saw the blood and no harm would come to them.

Of course, God knew the difference between the Egyptian and Jewish homes. This was actually a foreshadowing of the coming Christ; a lesson for his people then, and for the generations that followed. In John 1:29 we can see that John the Baptist fully understood this parallel: "The next day John saw Jesus coming toward him and said, 'Look, the Lamb of God, who takes away the sin of the world!'" And as if completing the thought, 1 Peter 1:19 describes Jesus as "a lamb without blemish or defect."

A PLETHORA OF PASSAGES POINT TO THE NARROW GATE

Despite what is believed by so many people in this postmodern culture, the way to heaven is truly that narrow. That's why the blood of Jesus, the perfect Lamb of God, provides the only way to salvation. It provides a covering so that eternal death will "pass over" us. I used to think there were maybe one or two passages of Scripture that pointed to this truth, but as I did a little research I found there are actually an overwhelming number of supportive references. I have listed many of them here, but please don't too quickly...uh...pass over them. They are critically important in understanding the true Gospel:

- John 10:9–"I [Jesus] am the gate; whoever enters through me will be saved."

- John 10:28–"I [Jesus] give them eternal life, and they shall never perish..."

- John 14:6–"I [Jesus] am the way and the truth and the life. No one comes to the Father except through me."

- John 17:2-3–"For you granted him [Jesus] authority over all people that he might give eternal life to all those you have given him."

- Romans 5:9–"Since we have now been justified by his [Jesus'] blood, how much more shall we be saved from God's wrath through him!"

- 2 Corinthians 5:21–"God made him [Jesus] who had no sin to be sin for us, so that in him we might become the righteousness of God."

After seeing these multiple Scriptures, it is hard for me to comprehend that anyone could continue to believe there is salvation apart from Jesus Christ. But here is one more passage that may say it best of all:

- 1 John 5:11-12–"And this is the testimony: God has given us eternal life, and this life is in his Son [Jesus]. He who has the Son has life; he who does not have the Son of God does not have life."

BELIEVING IS THE BEGINNING

For those who might have confusion as to what it means to "have the Son of God," it all begins with believing in Jesus and

His death and resurrection. As you'll see in these clarifying passages, this is *not* optional:

- John 3:16 -18–"For God so loved the world that he gave his one and only Son, that whoever believes in him shall not perish but have eternal life...Whoever believes in him is not condemned, but whoever does not believe stands condemned already because he has not believed in the name of God's one and only Son."

- John 3:36–"Whoever believes in the Son has eternal life, but whoever rejects the Son will not see life, for God's wrath remains on him."

- John 11:25–"Jesus said to her, 'I am the resurrection and the life. He who believes in me will live, even though he dies; and whoever lives and believes in me will never die.'"

- Romans 10:9-10–"That if you confess with your mouth, 'Jesus is Lord,' and believe in your heart that God raised him from the dead, you will be saved. For it is with your heart that you believe and are justified, and it is with your mouth that you confess and are saved."

ADDING IN OBEDIENCE

This last passage leads us into another important aspect of what it means to "have the Son of God." Yes it starts with believing, but even the demons believe in Jesus so there has to be more to it. That's probably why I cringe a bit when I hear the popular spiritual "math" equation: Jesus + Nothing = Everything. I understand what they mean; that salvation is by grace through faith in Christ alone. This is absolutely true. But I believe it's a virtual certainty that many people are hearing in that equation, "I believe in Jesus, so there is nothing else I have to do. I can live my life any way I please."

This is simply not true. Jesus fulfilled His responsibility by dying on a cross. Now we as Christians need to fulfill our responsibility by acting on our faith — both verbally and through our obedience. Again, this is *not* optional. Otherwise Jesus would not have made this important statement in Matthew 7:21: "Not everyone who says to me, 'Lord, Lord,' will enter the kingdom of heaven, but only he who does the will of my Father who is in heaven."

Among the other supporting Scriptures:

- John 8:51–"I tell you the truth, if anyone keeps my word, he will never see death."

- John 14:23-24–"Jesus replied, 'If anyone loves me, he will obey my teaching. My Father will love him, and we will come to him and make our home with him. He who does not love me will not obey my teaching."

- 1 John 2:3-5–"We know that we have come to know him if we obey his commands. The man who says, 'I know him,' but does not do what he commands is a liar, and the truth is not in him. But if anyone obeys his word, God's love is truly made complete in him."

This is coming straight from the Bible, and again, I would ask you not to pass too quickly over these verses. Maybe even consider reading them one more time. They are so crucial to a comprehensive understanding of the Gospel.

If Jesus is not both Savior *and* Lord of our lives, then we are liars and the truth is not in us. These are not my words, but the words of God as found in the Bible. And if we love Jesus and are obedient to His word, "God's love is truly made complete" in us and we will never see spiritual death.

Yes, salvation is by grace alone through faith in Jesus Christ alone. And if our heart's desire is to please Him and live for Him then we do have "everything." But if our lives do not reflect a genuine effort to be obedient to God's commands, then we need to take a serious look at the sincerity of our relationship with Him.

Now please don't misunderstand me. I know that all true Christians are tempted with sin on a daily basis. God simply wants us to do our best to live righteously. Then, even if we fall short many times, the blood of Jesus is sufficient to cover us. As 1 John 1:7 says: "But if we walk in the light, as he is in the light, we have fellowship with one another, and the blood of Jesus, his Son, purifies us from all sin."

CONCLUDING THOUGHT

There simply is no gray area when it comes to salvation. There is only one way to spend eternity with our loving heavenly Father — in a place where there will be no more death, mourning, crying or pain — and that's through Jesus Christ, the Narrow Gate. Acts 4:12 sums it up perfectly: "Salvation is found in no one else, for there is no other name under heaven given to men by which we must be saved."

I used to wonder why in God's design Jesus had to die in order to make provision for our salvation. After all, God made the rules. He could have come up with a different way that didn't grieve His heart. Instead, God had to watch as His beloved Son was beaten and tortured, and then crucified — a form of execution that was designed to be as painful as possible. (I know for me, I would gladly take such brutal treatment upon myself if it meant my daughters would be spared.)

Then one day during a prayer time at our church, a woman requested intercession for her wayward daughter. As we were praying, I looked up briefly and saw this heartbroken mother crying bitter tears for her child. And then it occurred to me — perhaps that is why God sent His only Son to die for our sins. There is a tenderness in the heart of a loving parent for their child that nothing can match. That is why some grieving parents simply never recover following the death of their child. And there is not a clear-minded, loving parent on earth that would willingly allow their child to go through an agonizing death if they had the ability to stop it. But that is exactly what God did.

Could it be that Jesus' torturous death was God's way of conveying the immeasurable extent of His love for us? He actually allowed His own Son to die for our sins! As it says in Romans 5:6-8:

> You see, at just the right time, when we were still power-less, Christ died for the ungodly. Very rarely will anyone die for a righteous man, though for a good man someone might possibly dare to die. But God demonstrates his own love for us in this: While we were still sinners, Christ died for us.

13–THE NARROW GATE: STILL WIDE OPEN

When you share your faith, it's very important to never take rejection personally. Whether you believe you handled the opportunity poorly or perfectly, God can use it for good. You may not see any immediate fruit, but it's your obedience that matters.

As I bring this book to an end, I'd just like to thank you for joining me on this journey to a better understanding of God's Word and His heart. I have dealt with some controversial issues through these pages and I know that some of my conclusions may be up for debate. But one thing we can know for sure is that the Narrow Gate to the Kingdom of God is still wide open. Second Peter 3:9 says: "The Lord is not slow in keeping his promise, as some understand slowness. He is patient with you, not wanting anyone to perish, but everyone to come to repentance."

I join God in having no greater desire than to see people come to a saving knowledge of Jesus Christ. Several years ago I came up with a strategy to share my faith; this was after I had developed friendships with many wonderful people who were not yet Christians. I came to care about them deeply and realized without Jesus, their eternity was tragically bleak.

What I would do is write them a personal note and put it in an envelope along with a tract idea I had. It turned out to be a well-received form of evangelism. After reaching out to them in this way, I never once sensed anything but appreciation. I'm sure it was apparent that I sincerely cared about their eternal destinies, whether they believed in what I shared or not.

For those of you who are Christians, I am including a sample of the personal note, as well as the "tract," so you can use them in your own evangelistic efforts should you so desire. I have written each of the notes over the years by hand (not on a computer) as a way of showing the person that I cared about them individually. Therefore the messages varied somewhat, and as I wrote I kept in mind the main reason we developed a relationship. For this sample, I'll pretend I'm writing to a neighbor.

Dear ***,
It has been a real pleasure getting to know you over the past several months. You have proven yourself to be a trustworthy neighbor and it is a real blessing to have someone nearby that I can count on when I need a hand.

You probably never expected to receive a letter from me, but there is something important that I would like to share with you. I have been a follower of Jesus Christ for many years, and as time has passed I have seen God reveal Himself to me as real, time and time again. I have come to completely trust in the Bible as His absolute truth, so when it says we need to believe in Jesus and His sacrifice on a cross in order to spend our eternity with God, I believe it.

If you were to die tomorrow I couldn't bear the thought of never having shared this important truth with you. If you are already a believer in Jesus, Praise the Lord! But if not, I have included a tract idea I had so that you can know what to do to become a Christian. Please read it with an open mind and then let me know if you have any questions. I would love it if we were neighbors in heaven someday as well!

Sincerely,
Randy Kennedy

I have also developed a strategy for some of the on-the-spot opportunities that God brings my way. This was prompted by a chance meeting at a truck stop along a freeway in Wisconsin. I had stopped to get gas, and as I went inside to pay there was a man sitting outside the entrance with a sign that read, "Need Money for Food." Like just about everybody else I basically ignored him as I walked past. But we did momentarily glance at each other, and as I drove away the hopelessness that I could see in his eyes in just that brief moment began to haunt me. After many miles I began to realize the Holy Spirit was revealing to me my insensitivity to this man's plight.

At that point it was too late to do anything other than remember him in my prayers. But I thought about how much of an impact it might make in the future if I could express my concern for such a person tangibly, both temporally and for eternity. So I have taken the simple step of putting separate envelopes in the glove compartments of our vehicles. In the envelopes I keep a $20 bill along with a copy of the tract idea. With that I have included a note that says:

> Here is money to help you with your need. I don't believe it was an accident that our paths crossed today. I believe God wanted me to prepare this envelope for you because He loves you. This is a temporary gift, but the gift of salvation is eternal. I've included a sheet that tells you how you can accept Jesus as your Savior. Please read it. I would love it if I end up seeing you again in heaven someday! Rest assured I will remember you in my prayers.

I originally started the note with the words "Here is money to buy some food" but I modified it after I ran across a man outside our church one Sunday afternoon who said he needed gas money. I was able to bless him with the $20, but the note wasn't pertinent. So the new, more generic note can fit a variety of needs.

On the outside of the envelopes I wrote the simple words, "God Bless You." I realize, depending on the situation, God could ask me to do more. And I also realize the recipient of the envelope could use the money to buy booze or something. But I have decided to leave that in God's hands. At the very least I will have done something that may eventually lead to eternal life for one more precious soul.

These are just a couple of ideas I have come up with in order to give God an opportunity to go to work. Of course, the possibilities are endless and perhaps you have come up with some ideas of your own. I find it very helpful to ask God daily for opportunities to share my faith, to help me be aware of the opportunities when they present themselves, and to give me the wisdom on how to handle those opportunities in the most productive way possible.

When you do share your faith, it's very important to never take rejection personally. Whether you believe you handled the opportunity poorly or perfectly, God can use it for good. You may not see any immediate fruit, but it's your obedience that matters. God may bring multiple Christians into that person's life before they finally submit to the prompting of the Holy Spirit. When I'm sharing my faith, I like to keep in mind the 1977 Keith Green song, "He'll Take Care of the Rest" (Sparrow Records). It contains some great words that really help take the pressure off:

> Just keep doing your best
> And pray that it's blessed
> And Jesus takes care of the rest

Next I have included the tract idea. If you are a Christian, feel free to copy it from this book to share with those you care about. If you are not yet a follower of Jesus, please read the tract with an open mind (as I said in the sample note) and consider joining the Kingdom of God. There is no better place to be, for now and for eternity.

WHERE WILL YOU GO WHEN YOU DIE?

The choice is actually yours. The Bible says that you will either spend eternity in heaven with God, or in a tormenting hell separated from God.

While many religions claim to know the way to eternal life with God, Jesus said in John 14:6, "I am the way and the truth and the life. No one comes to the Father except through me." A trip down the "Romans Road" will allow the truth of God's Word speak to your heart...

Romans 3:23 – for all have sinned and fall short of the glory of God

No matter how good you are, or how much good you have done, if you have sinned even once you have fallen short of the necessary holiness to live in God's presence

Romans 6:23–For the wages of sin is death, but the gift of God is eternal life in Christ Jesus our Lord.

The payment for your sin is an eternity in hell. But because of God's love for you, He made salvation available through His Son, who paid the debt for your sin by dying on a cross

Romans 10:9 – if you confess with your mouth, "Jesus is Lord," and believe in your heart that God raised him from the dead, you will be saved.

When you believe in Christ's sacrifice for your sins, and confess Him as your risen Lord, then you receive the gift of eternal life

The "Romans Road" reveals that an eternity with God is as easy as A,B,C

ADMIT THAT YOU HAVE SINNED – Tell God that you know you are a sinner, and that you are sorry

BELIEVE THAT JESUS DIED AS PAYMENT FOR YOUR SINS – Accept His sacrifice, and invite Him to be the Savior and Lord of your life

COMMIT YOUR LIFE TO HIM – Begin a practice of praying and studying the Bible daily, and start attending a church that believes in the Bible as the inerrant Word of God, so you can learn about Him and how He wants you to live

CONCLUDING THOUGHT

I was talking with a brother in Christ recently who said he had been discussing Christianity with his father. This elderly man told his son he didn't think he had any hope of salvation because he had spent his days living a life that was far from Godly. That very attitude convinced me there was hope, because the Holy Spirit was obviously still at work revealing this man's sin to him.

This conversation led me into the final thought I want to share. No matter where we have been, no matter what we have done, no matter how young or how old we are, there is still hope. If it is our own salvation we are concerned about, or the salvation of someone else we care about, as long as we are still on this earth it is not too late. The conversation between Jesus and the men who were crucified with Him provides a great example of this truth in Luke 23:39-43:

> One of the criminals who hung there hurled insults at him: "Aren't you the Christ? Save yourself and us!" But the other criminal rebuked him. "Don't you fear God," he said, "since you are under the same sentence? We are punished justly, for we are getting what our deeds deserve. But this man has done nothing wrong." Then he said, "Jesus, remember me when you come into your kingdom." Jesus answered him, "I tell you the truth, today you will be with me in paradise."

It didn't matter how this man had lived his life. His sincere "deathbed conversion" meant his sins were forgiven and he is now spending eternity in God's presence. Of course there is no wisdom in waiting; there is not even a guarantee we'll wake up tomorrow. But even if a person could predict when they would die, I will testify to the fact that there is no better way to live. Believers in Jesus have the peace of knowing that their sins are forgiven, that God is always there to care for them, and that a blessed heavenly hope awaits them for eternity.

I have heard it said that a gift is not yours until you accept it. For those who would choose to accept the priceless gift of salvation through Jesus Christ, even to this very moment, the Narrow Gate is still wide open!

ENDNOTES

1. Josh McDowell. *Evidence that Demands a Verdict* (San Bernardino, CA: Here's Life Publishers, 1979)

2. McDowell. *More Evidence that Demands a Verdict* (Here's Life Publishers, 1981)

3. Lee Strobel. *The Case for Christ* (Grand Rapids, MI: Zondervan, 1998)

4. Strobel. *The Case for Faith* (Zondervan, 2000)

5. *Why Trust the Bible?* (Torrance, CA: Rose Publishing, 2008)

6. Tim Mahoney. *Patterns of Evidence: The Exodus* (St. Louis Park, MN: Thinking Man Media, 2015)

7. C.S. Lewis. *The Lion, the Witch and the Wardrobe* (Nashville, TN: HarperCollins)

8. Brian Jones. *Hell is Real: But I Hate to Admit It* (Colorado Springs, CO: David C. Cook Publishing, 2011) 35

9. Dr. Neil Whitehead and Briar Whitehead. *My Genes Made Me Do It* (Lafayette, LA: Huntington House, 3rd edition, 2013) 267

10. Bruce Bickel and Stan Jantz. *World Religions and Cults 101* (Eugene, OR: Harvest House Publishers, 2005) 214

11. Dr. David Jeremiah and Carole C. Carlson. *Invasion of Other Gods* (Nashville, TN: Word Publishing Group, 1995) 107

12. Jeremiah and Carlson. *Invasion of Other Gods*, 123

13. Hank Hanegraaff. *The Complete Bible Answer Book* (Nashville, TN: Thomas Nelson, 2008) 297

14. Hanegraaff. *The Complete Bible Answer Book*, 298

15. Walter Martin, Jill Martin Rische, and Kurt Van Gorden. *The Kingdom of the Occult* (Thomas Nelson, 2008) 436

ABOUT THE COVER

The cover was intentionally designed with ambiguity. The center of attention is the doorway of a building that looks as though it could be either a church or a castle. Of course the church (the building) and the Church (God's people) are the focal points of His Kingdom on earth, just as a castle is the focal point of a man-made kingdom.

In the cover art, the structural integrity of the building and its doorway appear to have been compromised after years of damage caused by the surrounding elements. One of the weakened doors is ajar, indicating the building has been breached and invaders are inside. Unless these invaders are immediately exposed and removed, they may cause irreparable damage within the building through their evil intent.

Similarly, the structural integrity of the Church has been compromised after years of damage caused by the surrounding postmodern relativism. Because of the resulting disrepair, the doors are easily breached and invaders have been able to enter. Unless these invaders are immediately exposed and removed, they may cause irreparable damage within the Church through their false teachings.

KINGDOM INVADERS STUDY GUIDE

For best results, it is recommended that whenever possible group participants read each chapter prior to going through the study material

CHAPTER 1–THE BIBLE: CREDIBLE OR CORRUPTED

Comprehensive study of the Bible — as well as its related history, archeology, and other sciences – can provide confidence that it is indeed God's Word. It's true that you can't prove the Bible to be absolute truth, but you can get oh-so-close!

1. What are some of the ways we can know the Bible to be actual truth from God Himself?

- Amazingly, it was written over the course of sixteen hundred years by more than forty different authors from all walks of life — and yet a common thread is woven throughout

- To be included in the Holy Bible, the various books had to be recognized as inspired by a council of rabbis and councils of church leaders after passing a test of careful guidelines

- There is remarkable evidence that the Bible we have today is true to the original writings; more than fifty-three hundred ancient hand-made manuscripts still exist

2. What area of science provides the most convincing evidence that the Bible really is truth from God?

- Archeology regularly proves the accuracy of the Scriptures; never has any discovery ever disproved any aspect of the Bible

- The Dead Sea scrolls were found in 1947 in some caves in what is now called the West Bank of Israel; they were over one thousand years older than most manuscripts previously used for Bible translation and compared with them virtually word for word, proving the accuracy of the modern Scriptures

- More recent archaeological evidence points to a worldwide flood as described in Genesis 6-9; in Asia fossilized sea creatures have been located in the Himalayas, the highest mountain region in the world

3. What is the most compelling proof that the Bible is truly the Word of God?

- Literally hundreds of prophecies written in the Scriptures have been fulfilled

- Most of the Old Testament prophecies referred to the coming Messiah; no less than 109 of these prophecies were fulfilled by Jesus

- Probably the most amazing fulfillment of biblical prophecy relates to the nation of Israel (read Ezekiel 37:12-14); the Jewish people were dispersed from their homeland and scattered across the earth some two thousand years ago but became a nation once again, just as prophesied by Ezekiel around 580 BC

There are simply no other "holy books" used by any other religion that have provable authenticity like the Bible. On the contrary, archeology and other sciences have actually proven these other books to be contradictory and inaccurate at best, complete frauds at worst. And none of these other books can claim fulfillment of even a single specific prophecy, whereas literally hundreds of Bible prophecies have been, and continue to be, fulfilled.

CHAPTER 2–THE BIBLE: LITERAL OR LITERARY

(Read 2 Timothy 3:16,17) This passage makes it quite clear that the Bible is to be considered more than just a good book containing literary classics. Unfortunately, many who would call themselves Christians today think of the Bible in just that way — a piece of intriguing literature worthy of being known intellectually but hardly absolute truth.

1. The question of whether or not to take the Bible literally took on new life in the 1800's; what caused this to happen?

-	Charles Darwin and the theory of evolution began to gain credibility in the scientific community of the day

-	Because his theories appeared to be based on science, many Christians started to feel that their Bible-based creation theology must either be flawed, or the result of misinterpretation

-	So it was thought that in order for belief in Christianity to remain viable, evolutionary ideology had to be somehow integrated into the Bible's account of creation

2. What in the creation account of Genesis should convince us that even the most unbelievable stories in the Bible can be trusted as literal? (read Genesis 1:3, 6, 9, 11, 14, 20, 24, 26) What is the common denominator in these verses?

-	All God had to do was speak the words and this massive, complex universe was formed

-	This should be all we need to understand that absolutely *nothing* is impossible with God, including a literal seven-day creation week with literal 24-hour creation days

-	When you doubt this, the Bible becomes less authoritative from Genesis to Revelation, or worse, you start believing God doesn't really exist and the Bible becomes meaningless

3. What is another reason that people have a hard time accepting the Bible text as literal truth from God?

- Cultural differences between the Hebrews of the biblical era and we westerners of modern times can create some confusion when distinguishing between what is literal and what is literary

- For example, it was common practice among the Jewish people to use hyperbole, or exaggeration, to make a critical point (read Matthew 21:21)

- Jesus is not saying we can literally move mountains and have them thrown into the sea; the analogy is an obvious exaggeration used to emphasize the important point that the impossible is made possible through God

Another potential point of confusion when confronting the question of the Bible as literal or literary has to do with the fact that some portions are actually symbolic or poetic. But this shouldn't be a stumbling block because when this is the case, we are actually clued in. For example, the parables Jesus told were clearly just stories, but they were used as a very effective method of helping people understand biblical truth.

CHAPTER 3–AN INCONVENIENT TRUTH: HELL

The Scriptures relating to hell leave no doubt whatsoever that it does exist. That is unless you work very hard to create an alternate meaning. Unfortunately, this is what has happened in increasing measure in recent years. Many people, including some very prominent and influential Christian leaders, have come out with explanations for what hell is or isn't that are not biblical.

1. What is one prominent modern teaching that denies the existence of hell as a real place of eternal torment?

- The "hell as a trash dump" teaching says hell was actually, metaphorically speaking, a garbage dump that never stopped burning outside of Jerusalem (read Jeremiah 7:31-32)

- The name Valley of Ben Hinnom was translated from the Old Testament Hebrew word "ge'hinnom" which correlates with the New Testament Greek word "gehenna"; this was said to represent hell as merely a temporary place of earthly consequences for sin

- But the concept of ge'hinnom or gehenna was used so often as a synonym for hell that it was later understood to mean hell itself, and was translated as such in the New Testament manuscripts

2. What are some reasons that people have for coming up with alternative meanings for hell?

- The Calvinistic interpretation of election and predestination makes people believe that our free will does not enter into the equation (read Romans 8:29-33); but Peter, one of Jesus' closest disciples, makes it quite clear that being part of the elect is our choice and our responsibility (read 2 Peter 1:10-11)

- In the book of Matthew alone, hell is described as a place "where there will be weeping and gnashing of teeth" no less than six times; if you believe you or a loved one may be headed there, therein lies the desire to change hell into a kinder, gentler place

- Some people believe that a loving God would never send anyone to a place of eternal torment; but eventually there is a price to pay for rejecting Him (read Luke 12:4-5)

3. Do prominent Bible characters express belief in a real place called hell?

- Paul (read 2 Thessalonians 1:7-9)

- John (read Revelation 20:10); after that, there is what is called a Great White Throne Judgment in which those who have rejected God during their lives are thrown into the "lake of fire" along with Satan and his allies

- Jesus himself (read Matthew 18:8-9)

In understanding God's immeasurable love for us, it is insightful to look at all that He has done to *rescue* us from hell. God has given us His instruction manual, the Bible, to tell us all we need to know in order to be saved, and has sent His very own Son, Jesus, to die on a cross as payment for our sins. Would you be willing to allow your child to suffer and die if the choice was yours? Neither would I. But that's the kind of love God has for us.

CHAPTER 4–AN INCONVENIENT TRUTH: SATAN

Many Christians are beginning to believe Satan does not exist. And this thought is invading the Kingdom in increasing measure. Satan is propagating the lie because he knows that if you don't believe there is an enemy to battle, then you won't build your defenses, your guard will be down, and you won't be prepared to fight the spiritual battles when they come.

1. Which book of the Old Testament perhaps points to the reality of Satan better than any other?

- Job contains a remarkable "fly on the wall" look at the reality of Satan and his relationship with God; Satan wickedly chides God by saying Job is only a righteous servant because the hedge of protection placed around him has prevented him from facing any real hardship

- To prove Satan wrong, God allows him to inflict Job with all manner of trials and tribulations, including the loss of his possessions and livelihood, the death of his children, and the onset of painful sickness and disease

- Because Job remained faithful to God in the midst of his trials, he received earthly rewards double what he had before Satan's attacks

2. Which New Testament incident perhaps points to the reality of Satan better than any other?

- In both Matthew 4 and Luke 4 Satan meets up with Jesus in the wilderness, trying to tempt Him to sin before His earthly ministry begins

- Satan attacked Jesus in some of the same ways he goes after us, hoping to use pride, greed, and selfishness to entice Jesus into an act of iniquity; Satan tempted Jesus by twisting the Scriptures into saying what he wanted them to say

- Jesus overcame Satan's lies because He knew what the Bible *really* says — a great example for us

3. What peculiar phenomenon through the centuries perhaps points to the reality of Satan better than any other?

- From their enslavement in Egypt some thirty-five hundred years ago, to their captivity in Assyria and Babylon more than twenty-five hundred years ago, to their oppression under Roman rule during the time of Jesus, to the barbaric holocaust at the hands of Nazi Germany during World War II, the Jewish people have faced unjust persecution throughout history

- The Jews are God's "chosen people" (read Deuteronomy 7:6); that automatically makes them a target for Satan, who hates God and anyone He favors

- With a spirit-realm understanding, it is evident that Satan has always sought out and found willing vessels to attack, oppress, and even kill the Jewish people

When somebody does something sacrificially good, that is evidence of a supernatural godly influence in that person's life. Conversely, when somebody does what is evil, that is evidence of a supernatural satanic influence in that person's life. Make no mistake about it. Evil exists because Satan is real. There is really no other satisfactory explanation.

CHAPTER 5–GRACE GONE WILD: SOMETHING OLD

God's grace is a valuable and necessary component of our lives as Christians because we are imperfect people. We *need* grace. But when our understanding of God's grace is taken too far, it can be detrimental to the point of physical and spiritual danger; that is "Grace Gone Wild."

1. What belief popularized some five hundred years ago by John Calvin is helping to fuel the modern dilemma of Grace Gone Wild?

- "Eternal security" is a belief in which some denominations teach that once you proclaim Jesus as your Savior, then you are saved from that moment on no matter how you choose to live your life

- Other denominations have a different take on eternal security, teaching that once you are baptized as a baby or adult you are heaven-bound from that time on; this belief actually predated

Calvin by about twelve centuries, popularized in the late 300's AD by the influential bishop Augustine

- The belief in Grace Gone Wild tells us that God's grace trumps every other aspect of who He is; for instance, God is also a God of perfect justice

2. Is it possible to "lose" your salvation?

- (Read John 10:27-29) These verses would tell us "no" we can't lose our salvation

- But just as we chose to accept Christ, we can choose to reject him; the Parable of the Sower provides an example (read Matthew 13:20-21) Free will is not voided just because at one time a person professes faith in Christ

- The Holy Spirit is a gentleman who does not force Himself on anyone, He only comes to dwell in the person who invites Him in; similarly He will only stay where He is welcome

3. (Read Revelation 20:15) Can God's book of life be edited?

- The doctrine of eternal security would say that once a name is written in the book it can never be removed; but very early and very late in the Bible, we are told that the names of God's children which were once written in His book of life can be "blotted out."

- (Read Exodus 32:31-33) God made sure Moses knew that only the disobedient would be at risk of being removed from His book of life because of their choice to live in unrepentant sin

- (Read Revelation 3:4-5) From these verses, we see that God would not consider even for a moment blotting the faithful out of His book of life; conversely, it stands to reason that the opposite is true

Whether you believe in eternal security or not, this teaching has been used by some people to justify very sinful and destructive lifestyles. We must be wary of any grace-heavy teaching that gives permission to go against God's clearly expressed instructions in Scripture. Instead, we should embrace those things which inspire us toward a greater holiness and consecration to God.

CHAPTER 6–GRACE GONE WILD: SOMETHING NEW

A lot of what we hear from our Christian leaders these days is too heavy on spiritual "sweets." We are hearing the good stuff about grace, mercy, love, and forgiveness — which is absolutely critical to a proper understanding of God and the Christian life — but we are not being told enough about the other essentials needed to have a healthy, well-rounded theological diet. Among them is striving to live a life of obedience to God according to the Scriptures.

1. Is it healthy to have a "fear" of the Lord?

- (Read Psalm 103:11-13 and 17-18) Here, David draws a correlation no less than three times between God's love for His children and their appropriate fear of Him

- These verses are among many in the Bible pointing to the wisdom in having a healthy fear of the Lord; it is "healthy" because it is not a cowering type of fear where we have to be afraid of getting squashed by God if we displease Him

- A healthy fear of the Lord could be characterized as a respect with such depth that it would be unreasonable if it were reserved for anyone other than God Himself

2. What is one modern day belief that is helping fuel the dilemma of Grace Gone Wild?

- There has been a teaching around for several decades called the Prosperity Doctrine in which believers in Jesus are told that, as children of the King, they deserve the riches of the Kingdom; in other words, God loves us so immensely that He would want us to always be wealthy and happy — never requiring us to leave our comfort zone

- Rather than lead us to a life of progressive sanctification, in the end the Prosperity Doctrine and Grace Gone Wild basically turn Christianity into a more desirable set of beliefs — giving permission to read and know God's commandments and then ignore them, if we choose, to live the more abundant life as *we* see it

- But this does not reflect truth; Solomon was healthy, wealthy, and wise, and after taking advantage of all life had to offer, he found it to be "meaningless" (read Ecclesiastes 12:13) His words pretty well sum up what the Christian life should be all about

3. When a believer makes the grace of God into an object of worship similar to an idol, what tends to be the result?

- Their focus is often on emphasizing what we *can* do as Christians as opposed to what we *should* do as Christians; this type of mindset would logically prevent spiritual growth

- Those who are excessively focused on grace will often say this attribute of God will inevitably cause us to live obediently because we desire to show our gratitude to Him; but for a significant number of people this belief actually defies human nature

- In reality, even we as Christians are far more likely to do the right thing because we know inappropriate behavior leads to consequences

God's grace is immense and immeasurable, but those who persist in taking it for granted will eventually find it does have a limit. The opportunity to accept God's gift of salvation, His son Jesus, will one day come to an end. But no matter where a person has been or what they have done, if they repent of their sins with a sincere desire to please God, His grace is sufficient for them.

CHAPTER 7–DANGEROUS DECEPTIONS: HETEROSEXUALITY

There are certainly issues that can be considered "gray areas" where sincere Christians disagree based on their interpretation of Scripture. But there is simply no wiggle room when it comes to God's design for marriage and sexuality.

1. What is God's design for marriage and sexuality?

- (Read Genesis 2:22-24) Marriage is intended to be an unbreakable bond between the man and his wife; we can know for certain that this design was not meant just for Adam and Eve because, as the first people, they did not have any fathers or mothers to leave

- The polygamy of many Old Testament Hebrew patriarchs has often been used to dispute that marriage is only meant to be the union of one man and one woman; but each of these men faced serious consequences for their willing disobedience to God

- There is a similarity to these patriarchs today in that many who would call themselves Christians are being dramatically influenced by the culture around them; while polygamy is rare, many are still acting out sexually in ways that grieve the Lord

2. Isn't it unrealistic in this day and age to expect someone to abstain from sex until they are married?

- We live in a hyper-sexualized society where, even in our churches, otherwise very godly young females are wearing the shortest of shorts, skirts or dresses, and the tightest of pants; men have been designed by God to be visual creatures and need women to dress modestly

- Men can't possibly avoid all of the tantalizing visual stimuli, but it is not acceptable to sit there and stare, soaking it all in as long as possible; "look, but don't touch" is not good enough — God's instruction to men is "see, but don't look"

- We need to totally "reboot" how we go about our dating relationships as Christians or we will continue to fall short of what God requires; anything unmarried romantic partners do that causes sexual arousal should be immediately stopped because it cannot be satisfied in a godly way (read Song of Songs 2:7, 3:5, and 8:4)

3. Are there consequences to living together outside of marriage?

- The success rate for marriages that follow live-in relationships is actually very poor; depending on the study, statistics show that couples who cohabit before getting married are anywhere from 50 to 100 percent more likely to get a divorce than those who don't live together first

- When marriage is not honored as the exclusive place for sexual intimacy it has an impact on our mentality; there are elements of selfishness, insecurity, lack of trust, and questions of commitment that can either consciously or unconsciously invade the mindset of those who choose to live together

- A host of studies have also shown that life outcomes are far better for children raised in homes with a married father and mother; they are less likely to get in trouble in school, get pregnant in their teens, end up incarcerated at some point in their lives, and less likely to end up in poverty

The issue of pornography can help bring perspective to proper sexuality. If viewing porn is clearly a sin, then why would it be acceptable in any way to view the nakedness of a flesh and blood person in our presence? And if just seeing the nakedness of another is sinful, then why would we believe touching their bodies would somehow be all right? With these things in mind it would be absolutely absurd to consider total intimacy outside of marriage to be in any way acceptable in the eyes of God.

CHAPTER 8–DANGEROUS DECEPTIONS: HOMOSEXUALITY

As with the other forms of immoral sexual behavior, homosexuality has become more common in recent years. As it is gaining acceptance in the culture, Christians who would dare characterize homosexual activity as sinful are regularly being called "homophobic" and "haters." But speaking the truth in love as Jesus requires is not hateful.

1. What is the most destructive belief when it comes to homosexuality?

- If you believe they are born that way and are homosexual through no choice of their own, then naturally, accepting their lifestyle would be the most loving thing you can do; if homosexuality is defined by what they *are* as opposed to what they *do*, then certainly we would want to give them every relational and marital right that heterosexuals have

- But there has never been a scientifically verifiable study ever done that shows any genetic, hormonal, or physical difference between heterosexuals and homosexuals; on the other hand, no less than eight major studies of identical twins have shown that post-birth factors such as exposure to pornography or sexual abuse are by far the strongest contributors to homosexuality

- (Read 1 Corinthians 6:9-11) In verse 11, *were* is past tense, meaning that the people Paul was writing to were able to overcome and turn from their sin. If those who practice homosexuality were born that way, this would be an impossibility

2. What is the strongest physical evidence that man/woman sexuality is God's design?

- (Read Romans 1:26-27) Just like a nut and bolt are designed with a natural function that cannot be achieved separately, so too the anatomy of men and women indicate they have a function that can only be achieved together

- The rest of the biology surrounding sexuality points just as obviously to a master designer; through the union of their compatibly designed bodies, a human begins its life through the union of a man and a woman

- From start to finish, there is unquestionably a natural function for men and women that only works as designed by the creator, God himself

3. Why is so-called gay marriage a problem?

- The issue of same-sex marriage has actually become much bigger than simply a matter of gay rights; it is rapidly being used in our culture to draw a line in the sand as a way of punishing Christians who would stand up for biblical truth

- God's design for marriage can literally be found from Genesis to Revelation in the Bible (read Genesis 2:22-24)

- (Read Revelation 19:7) This points to one of the main spiritual reasons gay "marriage" is a problem; redefining marriage ultimately skews the proper understanding of Christ's relationship with His Church

Any act of sexual behavior outside of a one man/one woman marriage is sinful in the eyes of God so none of us has the privilege of being self-righteous. Does God love those who practice homosexuality? Absolutely. But can they continue in their behavior unrepentantly? Of course not. None of us is given permission to remain in our sin. We are expected to do all we can to forsake sinful lifestyles to the glory of God.

CHAPTER 9–THE BROAD ROAD: ISLAM

As with so many other dangerous beliefs, the thought pervading the culture that there are many ways to heaven is invading the Kingdom of God at the same time. This is despite the fact that the Bible contains many, *many* passages declaring that only through Jesus can we spend our eternity with God.

1. Apart from Christianity, what it is the largest and most influential spiritual belief in the world today?

- The founder of Islam is Mohammed, who was born in 570 AD in the land that is now Saudi Arabia; he learned much about Christianity and Judaism while growing up

- This is an important fact because the "revelations" he had written in the Qur'an contain many surahs, or chapters, that share common people and themes with the Bible; these apparent similarities have helped boost the false perception that Christians and Muslims worship the same God

- After Mohammed's death in 632 AD, Islam continued to grow as His followers continued to advance the religion through largely violent means; non-Muslims were forced to either convert, live in poverty, or be put to death

2. What is the true face of Islam — the violent terrorists or the moderate "peace-loving" Muslims?

- The early surahs written while in Mecca were quite genteel, compassionate, and inclusive; this was during a time when the fledgling religion was weak and struggling for acceptance

- The later surahs written while in Medina took on a more violent tone as Islam began to grow in numbers and in subsequent strength; Mohammed became a fierce warrior and began to spread his religion by the sword

- The Islamic doctrine of abrogation says when one surah in the Qur'an contradicts another, then the newer passage is considered better and replaces the previous passage; therefore the harsher, more violent Medinian surahs render the related, more peaceful Meccan surahs that were written earlier as null and void

3. What are among the "irreconcilable differences" separating the beliefs of Islam and Christianity?

- Muslims believe Jesus was a great prophet, but just one of many; and although the Qur'an says Jesus was born of a virgin named Mary, Muslims do not believe he was the son of God (read John 3:16-18)

- They also do not believe that Jesus died on a cross and rose again, but rather was rescued by Allah and taken to heaven (read 1 Corinthians 15:3-6)

- The Qur'an teaches that there are two angels assigned to every person to record their good and bad deeds; if their goods deeds outweigh their bad, then Allah *may* allow them into heaven; it is still up to his discretion (read Romans 10:9-10)

Simply put, in order to have eternal life you have to believe in Jesus as the Son of God, that He died on a cross for your sins, rose again, and then confess him as your Lord. Muslims believe none of this and therefore have not received salvation. With this in mind, Christians need to compassionately share the love of Jesus with Muslims, understanding that they have been imprisoned by a satanic deception

CHAPTER 10–THE BROAD ROAD: EASTERN RELIGION AND THE NEW AGE

Eastern religions, such as Hinduism and the closely related Buddhism, are having a major impact on the world today. Their influence among Western cultures has grown dramatically in recent years largely because of their acceptance as part of New Age Spirituality. These beliefs may seem harmless. But in the end, nothing could be further from the truth.

1. What is the utmost goal of Hinduism?

- Hindus desire to break free from the "individual soul" and unite with the "universal soul" (becoming one with the Ultimate Reality, the main god of Hinduism); this process is accomplished through the death/birth cycle of reincarnation and karma

- Reincarnation is the belief that after you die, you will be born again into a new life; that life will either be better or worse, depending on the good works and bad works you produced known as karma

- Among the methods used by Hindus to reach a mystical union with the universal soul are meditation and yoga; a guru named Patanjali created the techniques of yoga to divorce oneself from the material world and unite with the impersonal cosmic god of the universe, ultimately allowing the Hindu to escape the cycle of reincarnation

2. What is the utmost goal of Buddhism?

- Buddhists desire to achieve a godlike "enlightenment," overcoming the evils of greed, hatred, and ignorance through reincarnation; eventually, the realization of ultimate truth and understanding is achieved — an enlightenment known as nirvana

- While Hinduism is polytheistic with millions of gods, Buddhism is actually atheistic with no god; all spirituality is achieved through self-discovery and awareness

- Meditation is the central process by which Buddhists pursue nirvana; it is a practice, similar to Hinduism, in which a mantra such as "Om" is repeated over and over as a way of achieving mental calmness in an attempt to awaken a source of spiritual power from within themselves

3. What is New Age Spirituality?

- It is everything and nothing at the same time; many different religions and philosophical beliefs are welcomed in New Age Spirituality — including Christianity, Eastern religions, Native American practices, and psychic phenomenon — yet it is humanistic to the core

- The ultimate appeal of NAS is that it allows for a person to be "spiritual" yet tolerant and accepting of all beliefs, with no expectation of righteousness or obedience to God

- New agers are expecting a new world order — a coming global utopia created by a one-world government and a humanistic, unified religion; this belief is actually playing a role in fulfilling end times biblical prophecy (one-world government in Revelation 13:1-8, and one-world religion in Revelation 17:1-18)

The Bible says Satan is like a lion prowling around looking for someone to devour (1 Peter 5:8). Eastern religions, New Age Spirituality, and their related "tools" such as meditation and yoga effectively allow Satan an opportunity to pounce. These spiritual beliefs and their related practices have occultic roots. When combined with a modern naivete about their potential dangers, they clearly provide just the opening Satan needs to "devour" an unsuspecting life.

CHAPTER 11–THE BROAD ROAD: MORMONISM AND THE JEHOVAH'S WITNESSES

The followers of these prominent religions would claim to be Christians. But from their doctrines it is evident they cannot claim that title. They say their beliefs are based at least in part on the Bible, but what they believe and what the Scriptures teach have only a passing similarity.

1. What are some of the modern day evidences that Mormonism is based on a fraud?

- In the *Book of Mormon* written by Mormon founder Joseph Smith, the Native American people were purported to be descendants of the biblical Jews; modern DNA samples taken from Indian tribes in the Americas have uncovered virtually no Jewish blood, but rather, a highly-predominant Asian ancestry

- Portions of another "scriptural writing," the *Pearl of Great Price*, were supposedly translated by Smith from scrolls found with Egyptian mummies that he purchased from a traveling antiquities salesman in 1835; modern day Egyptologists have determined that the scrolls were not scriptural writings at all but merely remnants of common Egyptian funeral texts and related drawings

2. What are some "irreconcilable differences" between Mormonism and Christianity?

- Mormons believe that Father God, who rules the earth today, was once a man who became a god; he was conceived by another god who existed before him, who was conceived by another god who existed before him, etc. (read Isaiah 45:5)

- Father God and Mother God had millions of spirit children together; their firstborn was Jesus, followed by Lucifer, making them spirit brothers according to Mormon doctrine (read John 1:1-3) Jesus has always been part of the triune Godhead

- Mormons teach that there are three heavens — one for the faithful Mormons, one for the less-than-faithful Mormons and some exceptional non-Mormons, and one for non-Mormons who have been mostly bad; before entering this last heaven, these people must serve a temporary sentence in hell (read 2 Thessalonians 1:8-9)

3. What are some "irreconcilable differences" between the Jehovah's Witnesses and Christianity?

- Jehovah's Witnesses are taught that there is no Trinity; God has one name, Jehovah — Jesus is not the son of God, but rather, Michael the archangel — and the Holy Spirit is not part of the Godhead, but rather, an active force (read Genesis 1:26) This verse makes no sense unless God exists as a plurality

- Since they do not believe Jesus is the son of God, JW's are taught that his death on a stake (not a cross) only canceled out Adam's sin; this did however remove the curse of original sin, which allows them to achieve their own salvation (read Ephesians 2:8-10)

- Jehovah's Witnesses deny the existence of hell; they believe that all non-JW's evaporate after death, but a glorious afterlife awaits the faithful Jehovah's Witnesses — either in heaven or a rejuvenated earth

From this examination of a few key Mormon and Jehovah's Witnesses beliefs, it should be obvious that they are not at all Christian. The vast differences between their doctrines and what is taught in the Bible make any realistic attempt to reconcile them a practice in futility.

CHAPTERS 12 & 13–THE NARROW GATE

In God's design, there is saving power in the blood. When Jesus died on a cross, the blood He shed as the perfect, sinless "Lamb of God" provided a permanent sacrifice. That made atonement for sins a possibility for all of mankind for eternity. Despite what is believed by so many people in this postmodern culture, the way to heaven is truly that narrow (read Matthew 7:13-14).

1. What are some modern day evidences that there is power in the name of Jesus?

- Prayers which have been allowed for a couple of centuries in the United States — such as when politicians meet, or in schools at the start of the day or before their sporting events — now often face the court-ordered requirement that the name of Jesus can't be mentioned; why would this be unless there is something special and unique about that name?

- Areas of the world where Jesus' name is not honored are human rights train wrecks; in Communist countries — where atheism has been taught and encouraged — the rights of average citizens have been minimal, and in Muslim-dominant countries there have been many documented cases of injustices and atrocities

- During World War II, the Nazis effectively bullied the Christian church in Germany into silence, marginalizing their influence, and the brutality of the military in the Shinto-dominant country of Japan was also well-documented; conversely, the United States aided both Germany and Japan in recovery efforts after the war was over, likely influenced by the words of Jesus (read Luke 6:27) Such merciful actions by a conquering nation are rare in human history

2. (Read 1 John 5:11-12) What does it mean to "have the Son of God?"

244

- It all begins with believing in Jesus and His death and resurrection (read John 3:36) But even the demons believe in Jesus so there has to be more to it

- Jesus fulfilled His responsibility by dying on a cross; now we as Christians need to fulfill our responsibility by acting on our faith -- both verbally and through our obedience (read 1 John 2:3-5) One act of obedience is telling others about Jesus

- When you share your faith, whether you believe you handled the opportunity poorly or perfectly, God can use it for good; you may not see any immediate fruit, but it's your obedience that matters

3. Is the "Narrow Gate" still wide open?

- (Read 2 Peter 3:9) God's greatest desire is to see people come to a saving knowledge of Jesus Christ

- No matter where we have been, no matter what we have done, no matter how young or how old we are, as long as we are still on this earth it is not too late

- (Read Luke 23:39-43) This man's sincere "deathbed conversion" meant his sins were forgiven and he is now spending eternity in God's presence

There is no wisdom in waiting as there is not even a guarantee we'll wake up tomorrow; even if we could predict when we would die, there is no better way to live than with the peace of knowing our sins are forgiven, that God is always there to care for us, and that a blessed heavenly hope awaits for eternity.

CPSIA information can be obtained
at www.ICGtesting.com
Printed in the USA
FFOW05n1414011015